We Have Already Cried Many Tears

We Have Already Cried Many Tears

The Stories of Three Portuguese Migrant Women

Caroline B. Brettell

Southern Methodist University

WAVELAND

PRESS, INC.

Prospect Heights, Illinois

For information about this book, write or call:
  Waveland Press, Inc.
  P.O. Box 400
  Prospect Heights, Illinois 60070
  (847) 634-0081

Cover photograph courtesy of Dr. Paul Greenberg, Dallas, Texas.

ISBN 0-88133-878-8

Printed in the United States of America

7   6   5   4   3   2   1

Why does the cock always sing at four in the morning? Precisely at four he begins to sing. How can the cock count, how does he know the time? People of the village always regulate themselves by the cock, but no one has discovered why the cock counts like that. What intelligence does the cock have to sing right on time?

In the past, before there were watches, to know the time we always looked at the sun. My grandparents used to leave the door open so that the rays of the sun would pour into the house. They knew what time it was by the length of the rays. Others knew the time of day by the rising and setting of the sun and by the heat of the day.*

—The cock sings every day, the sun rises every day, and every day man meditates on his past which withdraws perpetually from the present; and on the present which enters into the future; and of the future, who knows?   C.B.

This is what life is—É isso a vida!*

Ricardina dos Santos

Table of Contents

APPENDICES

Preface 1995

This book is about three Portuguese women who migrated to France during the late 1960s as part of a massive exodus that had its origins in the need for labor in northern Europe in the post-World War II period. Although Portuguese men comprised the majority of emigrants to France in the early years, by the mid-1960s women began to leave their villages and urban neighborhoods in greater numbers. Some were married women who emigrated to join husbands already abroad, while others were single women who had heard about the lucrative employment opportunities that were available, particularly in domestic service.

The book's significance as a document of the experiences of female immigrants has perhaps assumed even more importance in the years since its first publication in 1982. In anthropology, as in the other social science disciplines, it was commonly accepted that the migrant, and especially the international migrant, was a young male who left his homeland for economic reasons. Migrant women were largely invisible. By the mid-1980s, however, the situation had changed. Numerous anthologies and case studies demonstrating the extensive role of women in both internal and international migrations of the past and the present had been published (Bhachu and Westwood 1988; Diner 1983; Ewen 1985; Gabaccia 1992, 1994; Gilad 1989; Grasmuck and Pessar 1991; Morokvasic 1984; Phizacklea 1983; Simon and Brettell 1986).[1] In fact, some migration streams, particularly those to the United States, have been dominated by women in recent years (Houstoun, Kramer and Barrett 1984).

The studies of migrant and immigrant women address a range of questions, among them their high labor force participation; the balance that is maintained between salaried employment on the one hand and domestic roles on the other; the implications of this balance for domestic relations and domestic power; the impact of migration on women's physical and mental health; and the differing attitudes of women by comparison with men to life abroad (Brettell and deBerjeois 1992). Many of these are issues that are raised by the three Portuguese women whose stories of migration are included here.

Although other young scholars have recently focused on Portuguese immigrant women in countries such as England (Giles 1991, 1992) and Germany (Klimt 1992), more attention has been given to the study of Turkish and North African women in northern Europe (Andezian 1986; Gerholm and Lithman 1988; Goodman 1987; Wilpert 1988), and particularly to the controversy surrounding practices such as the wearing of head scarves by Islamic school children (Beriss 1990) or the custom of female circumcision. By 1993 France had brought thirty families who had circumcised their daughters to court, an action that powerfully symbolizes the bicultural conflicts that can arise as a result of migration.

It is these same immigrant groups that have experienced recent racist attacks—for example, firebombs tossed into the homes of Turkish and Lebanese families in Germany by members of the neo-Nazi movement. Such incidents have drawn the attention of the media. In February of 1993 the *New York Times* ran a front page series on migrants who were "wearing out their welcome as their numbers grew" (Kamm 1993), and *National Geographic* in May of the same year published an article titled "Europe Faces an Immigrant Tide" (Range 1993). More recently, the *New York Times* noted that Italy, a country with a deep-rooted history of emigration, has become a receiving society and is having trouble handling the "reverse tide" (Tagliabue 1995).

The Portuguese in France have not been the object of these recent attacks and conflicts. They are generally recognized—as they were when I conducted my research twenty years ago—as European, Catholic, and "assimilatable." Indeed, Portugal is now a full-fledged member of the European Community and the country itself has changed significantly as a result of extensive investment and development. A Portuguese colleague of mine commented recently that he now knows how small his country really is: on the new highways that have been built with European Community funds, a drive from the northern city of Porto east to the border with Spain, which used to take ten hours, now takes three.

Like Italy, Portugal today receives immigrants, although in smaller numbers and largely from former Portuguese colonies and overseas territories. But it still also sends its people abroad. A few years ago, the nephew of Virginia, one of the women whose story of migration is included here, was working as a seasonal laborer in Switzerland. He left his village and his family for six months at a time. His motive was not unlike that of the men of the previous generation who saw emigration as the only way to accumulate the money necessary to build a new house.

In France the children of those who left Portugal in the 1960s and early 1970s are now adults making their own living. Some have returned to Portugal, including one of the daughters of Virginia's sister Rosa, but most have remained. Those born in France are citizens with

A village in the central interior of Portugal.

Virginia's nephew (now a migrant in Switzerland) holding the bladder of a pig after a pig killing.

the same rights and opportunities as the children of the French. In this regard, French law has consistently differed from that of Germany. While one can still find Portuguese women working in domestic service and as concierges, the younger generation have entered into clerical, health, educational, and government positions.[2]

When I launched this study of Portuguese immigrant women in the mid-1970s, only a few anthropologists, particularly Latin Americanists, had worked systematically on the problem of migration. Indeed, the political scientist who interviewed me for a Social Science Research Council grant wondered whether migrant workers in Paris was an appropriate topic for an anthropologist to study. European ethnography was still in its infancy, and the study of gender was represented by a single and adventurous publication, *Woman, Culture, and Society*, edited by Michelle Rosaldo and Louise Lamphere (1974).

Since that time, and particularly in the period since *We Have Already Cried Many Tears* was first published, the scholarship on immigrants in Europe has blossomed (Buechler and Buechler 1987; Boissevain and Vermeulen 1984; Castles, Booth and Wallace 1984; Grillo 1985; McDonogh 1993; Rex, Joy and Wilpert 1987), although there are still very few published works that help us enter directly into the lives of individual immigrants. Migration has become a central issue within anthropology (Brettell, forthcoming; Eades 1987; Kearney 1986), especially in relation to new theoretical trends that emphasize political economy, global processes and unbounded communities. The concept of transnationalism, which has recently been developed (Schiller, Basch and Blanc-Szanton 1992) to describe the participation of migrants in social fields that transgress geographic, political and cultural borders, could readily be applied to the Portuguese case. Although I was not working with this concept at the time that this book was written, clearly the three Portuguese women who recount their life stories are transnationals who not only travel back and forth with frequency to Portugal but also have property and family in their home communities with which they are intimately connected.[3]

If the literature on intra-European migration has grown, so too has the number of ethnographic studies of European populations, including those dealing with Portuguese culture and society (Bentley 1992; Cole 1991; O'Neill 1987; Pina-Cabral 1986). However, there are still too few studies of urban populations in Europe. While this is not the central emphasis of *We Have Already Cried Many Tears*, this book nevertheless shows how three women cope with life in a large capital city to which they have migrated for very different reasons. Migration is intimately connected to issues in urban anthropology (McDonogh 1993).

Additionally, feminist anthropology has reached maturity, recognized as a distinct subfield within the discipline (Brettell and Sargent 1993; del Valle 1993; di Leonardo 1991; Moore 1988; Morgen 1989). It is a subfield that has generated an extensive and rich library of ethnographies that documents the variability in women's lives in the diverse cultures of the world. These ethnographies not only explore the subjective experiences of women but also how these experiences are influenced by larger social, economic, political and ideological processes. It is precisely this dialogue between individual experience and macrolevel processes that is illustrated through the stories of the three migrant women presented here. The Portuguese and French states, through respective migration policies as well as other laws that determine basic rights and obligations, have impacted their lives. The same can be said for the ideological constructs of Portuguese womanhood that were partially shaped by the Catholic Church and an hierarchical system of social class.

In early feminist anthropology an opposition was drawn between the male public sphere and the female domestic sphere (Rosaldo and Lamphere 1974). This opposition, like the opposition between male honor and female shame that was described as characteristic of a Mediterranean cultural system (Peristiany 1965), has recently come under close and critical scrutiny (Lamphere 1993; Goddard 1994; Herzfeld 1980). Yet it is relevant, albeit in a negative sense, to the study of Portuguese women, whether in Portugal or abroad. The long history of male emigration in Portugal left women to carry out the agricultural duties of the peasant family (Brettell 1986). They have always been economically productive—a fact that leads Cole (1991) to emphasize the concept of the "worker" (*trabalhadeira*) as central to Portuguese female personhood. As one of the fisherwomen she interviewed said, "*Ser mulher é ser trabalhadeira.*" (To be a woman is to be a hard worker) (Cole 1991:33).

It would be very easy to argue that one of the most important contributions to anthropology that has emerged from European ethnography is in the study of gender roles and relations. The number of works are too numerous to cite, but among them are the explorations of gender, power and kinship in Greece by Dubisch (1986), and Loizos and Papataxiarchis (1991); the studies of masculinity in Spain by Brandes (1980) and Gilmore (1987); Giovannini's (1985) study of women factory workers in Sicily; and Harris's (1988) research on the impact of multinationals on women in Ireland. Perhaps the uniqueness of the Portuguese contribution to the literature on gender in Europe is the discussion of illegitimacy in relation to the codes of chastity and virginity that supposedly characterized the cultures of southern Europe. Illegitimacy is raised in this book through the story of Virginia, and indirectly (in the form of premarital sex) through the story of Ricardina. It is also addressed by Pina-Cabral (1986) and O'Neill (1987).[4]

I chose to present the material on Portuguese immigrant women in France through the words and experiences of three particular women. In doing so, I turned to the method of life history, a method that was particularly well developed in the study of Native American cultures. In the last decade, the life history has received renewed attention as a mode of writing and as a cultural text (Langness and Frank 1985; Peacock and Holland 1993; Watson and Watson-Franke 1985). One could almost argue that the life history has been "recentered" within anthropology as the discipline has become more reflexive and as theoretical trends have moved in the direction of rejecting a concept of culture that is equally shared by all members of a community.

Much of the impetus for the "revival" of the life history has come from within feminist anthropology, where an interest in hearing the voices of women has become a central concern (Abu-Lughod 1993; Behar 1990; Cole 1992; Geiger 1986). As Geiger (1986) has argued, life histories help us to gain access to the particularities of women's experiences under the changing political, economic and social conditions of the twentieth century. In addition, "they permit comparative cross-cultural studies of women's responses to such conditions in different settings" (343).

Many of the life histories of women that have been published during the past decade focus on a single individual, whether it is a Mexican marketing woman named Esperanza (Behar 1993), a !Kung woman named Nisa (Shostak 1981), an Irish tinker woman named Nan (Gmelch 1991), a Haida woman named Florence (Blackman 1982), a Korean shaman called Youngsu Mother (Kendall 1988), or a vodou priestess named Mama Lola (Brown 1991). These life histories differ in the manner and extent to which the ethnographer inserts herself in the text and comments on the words of the woman whose story is being told. While I sympathize with those who are critical of this authorial voice, I also believe that some cultural contextualization helps a reader to better understand the life story. Thus, I introduce each story with a description of the socioeconomic context that influenced a particular life, whether it is a rural village or an urban neighborhood in the city of Porto. I also comment on the key episodes in each life that I feel are part of larger cultural patterns. Finally, while some afficionados of the life history method might find these stories brief, I feel that it is important to describe the variations in women's experiences of migration. A single, more extended life history would not achieve this purpose.

At the end of the original edition of the book I included an afterword based on interviews with each of the three women five years after the original research. Since that time I have lost contact with Ricardina and Ana, but my friendship with Virginia has continued. Not surprisingly, the story did not end with what I wrote in the epilogue and "happily-ever-after" was not to be. In brief, her marriage did not work out. She lived with her husband, Manuel, in Venezuela for a time but he began a relationship with his secretary, a Venezuelan woman. The Venezuelan secretary became pregnant and Manuel eventually told Virginia he wanted a divorce. He wanted to marry the Venezuelan woman, move back to Portugal with her, and live on the *quinta* that he had purchased in 1980. He offered Virginia a small apartment in the city of Viana do Castelo.

Virginia felt that she had little choice but to agree. For a few years, particularly while her mother was still alive, Virginia hardly spent any time in the apartment. She found it lonely. When her mother died, however, family differences drove her from her natal household. Manuel provides her with some money each month, but it is insufficient. She has taken a job caring for an elderly woman five afternoons a week. One of Virginia's best friends is a woman named Amelia, someone she met while she worked in France. Amelia returned to Portugal and bought herself an apartment in Viana do Castelo. Amelia and Virginia are active in their local church.

Virginia's son, Joaquim, and her daughter-in-law, Iria, live in Portugal in a village to the west of Virginia's native village, but she rarely sees them. "My daughter-in-law thinks I am poor and uncultured," she once told me. Virginia would like nothing more than to see her grandchildren on a regular basis but is resigned to the fact that this is not to be. When I visited her a few years ago she readily admitted that some of the happiest times of her life were the years spent in France. "I had a kind boss and lots of friends."

Notes

1. In 1995, the Department for Economic and Social Information and Policy Analysis of the Population Division of the United Nations published a report titled *International Migration: Policies and the Status of Female Migrants*. The report was based on a conference held in San Miniato, Italy, in March of 1990.
2. For a fairly recent statistical analysis of female migration and foreign women in France, see Tapinos (1995).
3. Several scholars have criticized the tendency for anthropologists working in Europe to focus on small rural communities, isolating them in some sense from the outside world to which they are inevitably linked (Boissevain and Friedl 1975; Cole 1977; Grillo 1980). This tendency has been rectified in research carried out throughout the 1980s, which adopts an historical perspective and situates small communities in relation to national and global processes, including state formation (e.g., Maddox 1993; Verdery 1983).

Clearly, any study of migrants, especially one that adopts a transnational perspective, does not suffer from this small, isolated, rural community syndrome.

4. See Kelley (1991) for a discussion of unwed mothers in Spanish Galicia.

Bibliography

Abu-Lughod, Lila
    1993 *Writing Women's Worlds: Bedouin Stories*. Berkeley: University of California Press.

Andezian, Sossie
    1986 Women's Roles in Organizing Symbolic Life: Algerian Female Immigrants in France. In *International Migration: The Female Perspective*, edited by Rita James Simon and Caroline B. Brettell, pp. 254–265.

Behar, Ruth
    1990 Rage and Redemption: Reading the Life Story of a Mexican Marketing Woman. *Feminist Studies* 16(2): 223–258.
    1993 *Translated Woman: Crossing the Border with Esperanza's Story*. Boston: Beacon Press.

Bentley, Jeffery
    1992 *Today There Is No Misery: The Ethnography of Farming in Northwest Portugal*. Tucson: University of Arizona Press.

Beriss, David
    1990 Scarves, Schools, and Segregation: The Foulard Affair. *French Politics and Society* 8(1): 1–13.

Bhachu, Parminder and Sallie Westwood, eds.
    1988 *Enterprising Women: Ethnicity, Economy and Gender Relations*. London: Routledge.

Blackman, Margret
    1982 *During My Time: Florence Edenshaw Davidson, A Haida Woman*. Seattle: University of Washington Press.

Boissevain, Jeremy and John Friedl, eds.
    1975 *Beyond the Community: Social Process in Europe*. The Hague: Department of Education Science of the Netherlands.

Boissevain, Jeremy and H. Vermeulen, eds.
    1984 *Ethnic Challenge: The Politics of Ethnicity in Europe.* Gottingen:
        Herodot.

Brandes, Stanley
    1980 *Metaphors of Masculinity: Sex and Status in Andalusia Folklore.*
        Philadelphia: University of Pennsylvania Press.

Brettell, Caroline B.
    1986 *Men Who Migrate, Women Who Wait: Population and History in a
        Portuguese Parish.* Princeton: Princeton University Press.
    forthcoming Migration. *The Encyclopedia of Cultural Anthropology,*
        edited by David Levinson and Melvin Ember. Lakeville, CT:
        American Reference Publishing Inc.

Brettell, Caroline B. and Patricia A. deBerjeois
    1992 Anthropology and the Study of Immigrant Women. In *Seeking
        Common Ground: Multidisciplinary Studies of Immigrant Women in
        the United States,* edited by Donna Gabaccia, pp. 41–64.
        Westport, CT: Greenwood Press.

Brettell, Caroline B. and Carolyn Sargent
    1993 *Gender in Cross-Cultural Perspective.* Englewood Cliffs, NJ:
        Prentice-Hall.

Brown, Karen McCarthy
    1991 *Mama Lola: A Vodou Priestess in Brooklyn.* Berkeley: University of
        California Press.

Buechler, Hans Christian and Judith-Maria Buechler, eds.
    1987 *Migrants in Europe: The Role of Family, Labor, and Politics.* New
        York: Greenwood Press.

Caspari, Andrea and Wenona Giles
    1986 Immigration Policy and the Employment of Portuguese Migrant
        Women in the UK and France: A Comparative Analysis. In
        International Migration: The Female Experience, edited by Rita
        James Simon and Caroline Brettell, pp. 152–177. Totowa, NJ:
        Rowman and Allenheld.

Castles, S., H. Booth and T. Wallace
    1984 *Here for Good: Western Europe's New Ethnic Minorities.* London:
        Pluto Press.

Cole, John
    1977 Anthropology Comes Part Way Home: Community Studies in
         Europe. *Annual Review of Anthropology* 6:349–378.

Cole, Sally
    1991 *Women of the Praia: Work and Lives in a Portuguese Coastal
         Community.* Princeton: Princeton University Press.
    1992 Anthropological Lives: The Reflexive Tradition in a Social
         Science. In *Essays on Life Writing: From Genre to Critical Practice,*
         edited by Marlene Kadar, pp. 113–127. Toronto: University of
         Toronto Press.

del Valle, Teresa
    1993 *Gendered Anthropology.* London: Routledge.

di Leonardo, Micaela
    1991 *Gender at the Crossroads of Knowledge: Feminist Anthropology in
         the Postmodern Era.* Berkeley: University of California Press.

Diner, Hasia
    1983 *Erin's Daughters in America: Irish Women in the Nineteenth
         Century.* Baltimore and London: The Johns Hopkins University
         Press.

Dubisch, Jill, ed.
    1986 *Gender and Power in Rural Greece.* Princeton: Princeton
         University Press.

Eades, Jeremy, ed.
    1987 *Migrants, Workers, and the Social Order.* London: Tavistock
         Publications.

Ewen, Elizabeth
    1985 *Immigrant Women in the Land of Dollars, 1820–1929.* New York:
         Monthly Review Press.

Gabaccia, Donna
    1994 *From the Other Side: Women, Gender, and Immigrant Life in the
         U.S. 1820–1990.* Bloomington: Indiana University Press.

Gabaccia, Donna, ed.
    1992 *Seeking Common Ground: Multidisciplinary Studies of Immigrant
         Women in the United States.* Westport, CT: Greenwood Press.

Geiger, S.
   1986 Women's Life Histories: Method and Content. *Signs* 11:334–351.

Gerholm, Tomas and Yrigue Lithman, eds.
   1988 *The New Islamic Presence in Europe.* London: Mansell Publishing Company.

Gilad, Lisa
   1989 *Ginger and Salt: Yemeni Jewish Women in an Israeli Town.* Boulder: Westview Press.

Giles, Wenona
   1991 Class, Gender and Race Struggles in a Portuguese Neighborhood in London. *International Journal of Urban and Regional Research* 15(3): 432–441.
   1992 Gender, Inequality and Resistance: The Case of Portuguese Women in London. *Anthropological Quarterly* 65(2): 67–79.

Gilmore, David
   1987 *Aggression and Community: Paradoxes of Andalusian Culture.* New Haven: Yale University Press.

Giovannini, Maureen
   1985 The Dialectics of Women's Factory Work in a Sicilian Town. *Anthropology* 9(1/2): 45–64.

Gmelch, Sharon
   1991 *Nan: The Life of an Irish Travelling Woman.* Prospect Heights, IL: Waveland Press.

Goddard, Victoria A.
   1994 From the Mediterranean to Europe: Honour, Kinship and Gender. In *The Anthropology of Europe: Identities and Boundaries in Conflict,* edited by Victoria A. Goddard, Josep R. Llobera and Cris Shore, pp. 57–92. Providence: Berg Publishers Ltd.

Goodman, Charity
   1987 Immigrant and Class Mobility: The Case of Family Reunification Wives in East Germany. *Women's Studies* 13:235–248.

Grasmuck, Sherri and Patricia R. Pessar
   1991 *Between Two Islands: Dominican International Migration.* Berkeley: University of California Press.

Grillo, Ralph
    1985 *Ideologies and Institutions in Urban France: The Representation of Immigrants*. Cambridge: Cambridge University Press.

Grillo, Ralph, ed.
    1980 *Nation and State in Europe: Anthropological Perspectives*. London: Academic Press.

Harris, L.
    1988 Women's Response to Multinationals in County May. In *Women and Multinationals in Europe*, edited by D. Elson and R. Pearson. London: Macmillan.

Herzfeld, Michael
    1980 Honor and Shame: Problems in the Comparative Analysis of Moral Systems. *Man* 16:339–351.

Houstoun, M. F., R. G. Kramer, and J. M. Barrett
    1984 Female Predominance of Immigration to the United States Since 1930. *International Migration Review* 18:908–963.

Kamm, Henry
    1993 Migrants Wear Out Welcome as Numbers Grow in Europe. *New York Times*, February 10, p. 1.

Kearney, Michael
    1986 From the Invisible Hand to Visible Feet: Anthropological Studies of Migration and Development. *Annual Review of Anthropology* 15:331–404.

Kelley, Heidi
    1991 Unwed Mothers and Household Reputation in a Spanish Galician Community. *American Ethnologist* 18(3): 565–580.

Kendall, Laurel
    1988 *The Life and Hard Times of a Korean Shaman: Of Tales and the Telling of Tales*. Honolulu: University of Hawaii Press.

Klimt, Andrea
    1992 *Temporary and Permanent Lives: The Construction of Identity Among Portuguese Migrants in Germany*. Unpublished Dissertation, Department of Anthropology, Stanford University.

Lamphere, Louise
  1993 The Domestic Sphere of Women and the Public World of Men:
       The Strengths and Limitations of an Anthropological
       Dichotomy. In *Gender in Cross-Cultural Perspective*, edited by
       Caroline B. Brettell and Carolyn F. Sargent, pp. 67–77.
       Englewood Cliffs, NJ: Prentice-Hall.

Langness, L. L. and Gelya Frank
  1985 *Lives: An Anthropological Approach to Biography*. Novato, CA:
       Chandler and Sharp.

Loizos, Peter and Evthymios Papataxiarchis, eds.
  1991 *Contested Identities: Gender and Kinship in Modern Greece*.
       Princeton: Princeton University Press.

MacDonald, Sharon, ed.
  1993 *Inside European Identities: Ethnography in Western Europe*.
       Providence: Berg Publishers.

McDonogh, Gary W.
  1993 The Face Behind the Door: European Integration, Immigration,
       and Identity. In *Cultural Change and the New Europe:
       Perspectives on the European Community*, edited by Thomas M.
       Wilson and M. Estellie Smith, pp. 143–166. Boulder: Westview
       Press.

Maddox, Richard
  1993 *El Castillo: The Politics of Tradition in an Andalusian Town*.
       Urbana: University of Illinois Press.

Mandel, Ruth
  1994 Fortress Europe and the Foreigners Within: Germany's Turks. In
       The Anthropology of Europe: Identities and Boundaries in Conflict,
       edited by Victoria A. Goddard, Josep R. Llobera and Cris Shore,
       pp.113–124. Providence: Berg Publishers Ltd.

Moore, Henrietta
  1988 *Feminism and Anthropology*. Minneapolis: University of
       Minnesota Press.

Morgen, Sandra, ed.
1989 *Gender and Anthropology: Critical Reviews for Research and Teaching*. Washington, DC: American Anthropological Association.

Morokvasic, Mirjana
1984 Birds of Passage Are Also Women. *International Migration Review* 18(4): 886–907.

O'Neill, Brian
1987 *Social Inequality in a Portuguese Hamlet*. Cambridge: Cambridge University Press.

Peacock, James L. and Dorothy C. Holland
1993 The Narrated Self: Life Stories in Process. *Ethos* 21(4): 367–383.

Peristiany, John, ed.
1965 *Honour and Shame: The Values of Mediterranean Society*. London: Weidenfeld and Nicolson.

Phizacklea, Annie, ed.
1983 *One Way Ticket: Migration and Female Labour*. London: Routledge and Kegan Paul.

Pina-Cabral, Joao de
1986 *Sons of Adam, Daughters of Eve: The Peasant World View of the Alto Minho*. Oxford: Clarendon.

Range, Peter Ross
1993 Europe Faces an Immigrant Tide. *National Geographic* 183(5): 94–124.

Rex, John, Daniel Joy and Czarina Wilpert, eds.
1987 *Immigrant Associations in Europe*. London: Gower Aldershot.

Rosaldo, Michelle Z. and Louise Lamphere, eds.
1974 *Woman, Culture, and Society*. Stanford: Stanford University Press.

Schiller, Nina Glick, Linda Basch and Cristina Blanc-Szanton, eds.
1992 *Towards a Transnational Perspective on Migration: Race, Class, Ethnicity, and Nationalism Reconsidered*. New York: New York Academy of Sciences.

Shostak, Marjorie
1981 *Nisa: The Life and Words of a !Kung Woman*. Cambridge: Harvard University Press.

Simon, Rita James and Caroline B. Brettell
1986 *International Migration: The Female Experience*. Totowa, NJ: Rowman and Allenheld.

Tagliabue, John
1995 Sunny Italy Turns a Scowling Face to Immigrants. *New York Times*, January 5, p. 4.

Tapinos, Georges P.
1995 Female Migration and the Status of Foreign Women in France. In *International Migration Policies and the Status of Female Migrants*. New York: United Nations.

Verdery, Katherine
1983 *Transylvania Villagers: Three Centuries of Political, Economic, and Ethnic Change*. Berkeley: University of California Press.

Watson, Lawrence C. and Maria-Barbara Watson-Franke
1985 *Interpreting Life Histories: An Anthropological Inquiry*. New Brunswick, NJ: Rutgers University Press.

Wilpert, Czarina
1988 Migrant Women and Their Daughters: Two Generations of Turkish Women in the Federal Republic of Germany. In *International Migration Today: Emerging Issues*, edited by Charles Stahl, pp. 168–186. Paris: UNESCO.

Acknowledgments

I owe my deepest gratitude to Ricardina dos Santos, Virginia Caldas, and Ana Rodrigues, for without their frank and patient support, this volume could never have been conceived. Their willingness to share their lives and experiences with me is only one small indication of the generosity and kindness characteristic of most of their compatriots.

I would also like to thank the Social Science Research Council, the Canada Council, and the Gulbenkian Foundation for their munificent financial assistance at various stages of the research. The material on which this volume is based was gathered while I was conducting fieldwork in Paris and northern Portugal on the role of women in Portuguese migration to France.

I am extremely grateful to Louise Lamphere, who has consistently encouraged me in my work on female migration; to Philip Leis, who guided me through my first major fieldwork experience; to George Hicks, who has been a very helpful critic; and to Joyce Riegelhaupt, Maria Beatriz Rocha Trindade, and Colette Callier-Boisvert, all of whom have been good colleagues and friends. I want to express particular appreciation to Dr. Elina Guimarães, who shared some of her personal experiences with me and who has supported the Portuguese feminist cause with her courage and energy for over fifty years. The names of other people in Portugal and France who helped me at different times and in different ways are too numerous to list. They know who they are and I thank them.

Francis Milfeld and Pamela Hurd shared in the labors of typing the final manuscript. I am grateful to them and to my other friends and colleagues at the Population Research Center of the University of Texas who have provided a quiet and congenial atmosphere for writing and research.

Finally, this book is dedicated to the three most important people in my life: my mother, who has always encouraged me to write; my father, whose inquiring mind has always served as an example; and my husband Rick, who cheerfully shared all the trials and joys of ethnographic fieldwork. To each of them, *muito obrigada!*

General Map of Portugal
Showing Places of Origin of Three Women

Introduction

Sociologists and anthropologists approach and perceive man differently; they have different *images of man*. In his search for laws and his interest in the abstract, the sociologist tends to view man as a technically "non-human" item subject to many forces (including the sociologist's impersonal measurements). In this view, man is an element of nature, immersed in his environment—the sociologist stands apart observing and measuring man-in-environment.

For the anthropologist, man is not a figure within a ground, but rather a figure against that ground; he is a *human* phenomenon, everlastingly variable, predictable only within broad limits, if at all, and knowable on a series of virtually infinite levels of understanding. While the sociologist proposes to stand away, to perceive man "objectively," not to involve his own feelings and reactions, the cultural anthropologist has often striven to know man *through* his own feelings and reactions, to view the human beings he studies as fellow men, not as subjects.

John Bennett and Kurt Wolff
"Toward Communication between
Sociology and Anthropology"

I. CULTURE AND THE INDIVIDUAL: THE USE OF NARRATIVES IN ANTHROPOLOGICAL RESEARCH

Among social scientists, anthropologists are frequently the object of attack for their lack of rigor, their subjectivity, and their insufficient attention to quantification. As a result, they have turned increasingly to quantitative methods of data collection and analysis; yet it remains true that some of their best material is still gathered from a handful of individuals who lead them into the complex inner world of another culture. Some of these individuals are more adept than others at this task, better at describing and explaining themselves or the way of life of which they are a part. They become "key informants," but also friends, and they epitomize the Janus-like role of the anthropologist as both stranger and friend. This role has formed the basis for much methodological, even epistemological, discourse in the field—discourse focusing on how the anthropologist gains information, how valid this information is, how representative it is, and finally, how it is to be presented. Nowhere is this discussion more apparent than in the body of literature addressing the use of life histories, case studies, or even key informants. Obviously, these questions are of extreme importance to the present volume which seeks to tell the reader something about Portuguese women and their role in migration through the lives and experiences of three individual women who emigrated to France in the late 1960s.

I confess that one reason for choosing the biographical format is that it satisfies my wish to present ethnographic data in a readable, perhaps even literary, style and to communicate, if only impressionistically, the humanistic side of anthropology. However, there are other reasons for choosing this format—reasons related to theoretical and methodological issues in both migration studies and anthropology.

Although any consideration of the role of women in migration necessarily recognizes the importance of broad macroeconomic and demographic factors associated with labor movements, it also makes it possible to emphasize some of the human motives and decisions associated with geographic dislocation within or across national boundaries. Constance Cronin, in a study of Italians in Australia, was extremely insightful in insisting that it is ultimately individuals, or at most families who migrate; not cultures, societies, or even social groups. Yet the theoretical models of migration that have been and continue to be developed in academic scholarship are based largely upon aggregate analyses of population movement by age, sex, marital status, education, or economic position. Consequently, we still know little about the dynamics of human decision making with respect to migration. To establish the push-pull of socioeconomic or political factors that encourage migration is one thing; to establish the personal or familial circumstances that explain why any single individual migrates is quite another. Furthermore, it is important to realize that neither the decision-making process nor the actual migration are easily observable phenomena. Thus we must rely on detailed accounts of particular individuals—accounts which are by their very nature personal. These accounts can then be cast against a larger social, cultural, economic, and political background in which significant migration occurs.

The stories of Ricardina dos Santos, Virginia Caldas, and Ana Fernandes contribute to a greater understanding of the way in which the decision to migrate is made and how this decision fits into a life strategy. Although each of the stories is different, they all show that, given a context in which migration is a definite life-course option, the final decision to depart is made in response to a particular event or series of events in the individuals' lives. These events have little to do with the economic motives normally associated with international migration, despite the fact that the post facto explanation for the move is abridged in the vaguely economic phrase *para melhorar a vida* ("to make a better life").

This provides one theoretical reason for emphasizing the individual in studies of migration. There is, however, a second reason which is both theoretical and methodological. Working with the problem of migration has meant working, for the most part, in urban environments. For the anthropologist, this has necessitated a reevaluation of research methods that were developed to study small-scale, easily boundable, and largely rural societies. Essentially, two avenues were open to the so-called urban anthropologist who wished to continue the face-to-face, participant-observation style of data collection fundamental to the holistic ethnological perspective. One choice was to find, in the city, a geographically or socially identifiable "group" or "community"; the other was to work with individuals and with their personal social networks. The impact of these two approaches upon theoretical developments in urban anthropology is apparent in research on urbanizing Africa which has produced studies as different as Plotnicov's *Strangers to the City* and Cohen's *Custom and Politics in East Africa*.

To a certain extent, the problem that the researcher wishes to address influences the choice of methods. However, it is also possible to argue that the character of the urban environment is equally significant. In my study of Portuguese migrant women in Paris—the study from which material for this book is drawn—both factors were instrumental in defining an approach that focused on individuals rather than on a community or a subculture. First, unlike those anthropologists who are interested in tracing migrants from a single rural community to the city, or in studying a residentially segregated ethnic population (both cases of identifiable social *groups*), I was interested in studying a broad social *category*—Portuguese women, and a social process—migration—in which each individual participates somewhat differently. Variations were fundamental to the range of experiences I hoped to explore. Second, for a number of reasons related to an essentially assimilationist immigration policy, to the structure of the city of Paris itself, and to the nature of migrant female employment,[1] there is no localized "little Portugal" that has chiseled out its own social niche within the French capital metropolis. Portuguese migrants in Paris interact individually, or at most as a family, with the city and with French society rather than through the buffer zone that an ethnic community might provide. Some are better integrated than others and the differences among them must be traced with reference to individual migration strategies and unique processes of social adjustment or adaptation.

The dialectical tension between a "culture" and the "individual" is problematic both theoretically and methodologically in studies of migration. This tension is also at the very heart of debates over the use of life-history or case-study material in anthropological research. The origins of such personal documents are to be found in early ethnographic studies of the American Indian where anthropologists were essentially faced with the work of recovering evanescing cultures. One of the primary methods used was to record the life histories of the few available individuals who could articulate the traditional way of life or provide an inside view. The results were such classics as Radin's *Crashing Thunder* (1926), Dyk's *Son of Old Man Hat* (1938), Ford's *Smoke from their Fires* (1941), and Simmons's *Sun Chief* (1942). To a certain extent, migrants living in a foreign country who are asked to talk about the culture and society they have left are performing a task similar to that performed by these early American Indian informants. Both are describing cultures at a distance, although in one case that distance is measured more by the passing of time and in the other, more by the traversing of space.

Simultaneous with the collection and presentation of some of these early Indian life histories, a series of discussions arose about the contributions that autobiographical and biographical studies could make to anthropology in general. In these more theoretically oriented writings, the culture-individual dialectic was more formally addressed. The ethnographer-ethnologist was pitted against the so-called psychological anthropologist of the newly formed "culture and personality" school.[2] While the former was primarily interested in using life-history material as a means to describe or portray a culture, the latter was interested in it as a means to elucidate distinctive personality types. In other words, there was a fundamental difference between those who were concerned with the "facts" of a report as opposed to those who were concerned with what a report might reveal about the perceptions, motivations, and cognitive world of the individual reporter.

These two approaches are not totally irreconcilable, however. In recounting some aspect of his or her own life, an individual can make statements that have both cultural and personal import, and it is the job of the ethnologist to distinguish and interpret the two. This is precisely what Dollard noted in his discussion of a passage in *Crashing Thunder* where a culturally acceptable response is juxtaposed quite clearly with private "actual" feelings.

> Some time after this we found that my wife had married again. I did not feel like eating, but I tried hard to do so because I thought that the others would notice it. Then I said I am glad to hear that it is reported that my wife has married again. When I get out of prison, I will pay the one who has [married her] for he is going to take care of her until I get out. I had been quite uneasy about her for some time, and now I feel quite relieved, for she is going to be taken care of. Thus I said . . . but the truth of it was that I was about as angry as I could be. I made up my mind that I would take her away from whomever she might be living with. Then I thought that I would make her feel as sad as I could. I thought that I would disfigure her and leave her.[3]

What Dollard perceived in pointing to this passage is elaborated further by Goodenough who has defined three separate cultures: private, generalized, and public. Private culture refers to an individual's personal outlook, his or her subjective view of the world and its contents. Generalized culture is what we refer to when we speak of the culture of a community, but because it is always part of someone's private culture it differs from one individual to another. Finally, to the extent that consensus develops over the content of generalized and private cultures, a group may be said to have a public culture, "a culture that its members share and that belongs to all of them as a group."[4] Bringing Goodenough to bear upon the use of personal informants' accounts or life histories, the degree to which these documents are typical or representative depends upon the level of analysis at which they are interpreted and individual variations are as important as what individuals have in common.

It is within this kind of framework that the stories of Ricardina dos Santos, Virginia Caldas, and Ana Fernandes are presented. Each woman was approached initially to talk about her own life and her own experiences as a migrant. As the accounts developed, however, they all began to make statements that were best handled with reference to a larger socioeconomic and cultural context. My ultimate task, therefore, has been to knit these three separate accounts together into a single picture that reveals something about the lives of Portuguese women and about their role in migration, without losing sight of the specific situations, feelings, perceptions, and reactions that make each account unique.

This leads me to the matter of why these three particular stories were chosen. Before addressing that question, it is worth noting that when anthropologists have collected life histories, they have normally concentrated on a single individual, and it is largely for this reason that the method itself has come under attack—that is, where questions about the "typicalness" of the individual chosen (and therefore questions about representativeness and validity) are raised. There are, however, two good examples where a multiple story approach has been adopted. One is, of course, Lewis's work in *The Children of Sanchez* and *La Vida*: he puts together the separate accounts of members of a single family in which we often see each family member relating a similar event from his or her own perspective and with his or her own interpretation. Lewis is more interested in these separate interpretations than he is in discovering "what the truth really is." Indeed, if there is some way of knowing "what the truth really is," then it is more interesting to explore why this truth has been misrepresented by any single individual. In other words, Lewis's work raises the question of whether validity has its place in anthropology, or at least whether it is a fruitful measure of the accuracy of anthropological statements.

A second and more recent use of multiple life histories is Kelley's research on Yaqui women: she collected narratives from approximately twenty-five women within an extended kin group and then selected four to present in her study because they were the fullest and because they represented a range of experiences. Both of Kelley's reasons for selecting the particular life histories that she includes in her book are equally applicable to my choice of the narratives of Ricardina, Virginia, and Ana from the forty accounts I collected during a year of research in Paris.

All three women took a keen interest in the study and volubly recounted stories that were among the most complete. Not only did they discuss in detail the reasons for their own emigration to France, but each of them, by describing aspects of her childhood and youth, helped me to understand more fully the experiences of lower-class women in Salazarist Portugal. However, beyond the richness of their stories, there is a more deliberate and analytical reason for the choice of these three narratives. They represent distinct patterns of migration for women at various stages of the life cycle. In addition, each of the women comes from a different socioeconomic background. Taken together, they remind us, at the very least, of the pervasiveness of emigration in Portuguese culture. At most, they afford an opportunity to contrast and compare the lives of women in different sectors of Portuguese society and the varying experiences that are both a cause and a result of migration.

Ricardina was born in a hamlet in the interior of Portugal. In her narrative, she describes what life was like for a young girl growing up in a small, rural, out-of-the-way place where there is still no electricity and which is accessible only by a very poor, dirt road. She emigrated as a young, single woman, married in France, and has borne both her sons abroad. Many other Portuguese women have found themselves in similar circumstances, adjusting simultaneously to life as a migrant and as a wife and mother.

Virginia comes from a rural background as well, but her native village is in the northern coastal region of Portugal. It is a larger, more economically diverse, and more "modernized" village located on a major thoroughfare between two important provincial towns. She also emigrated as a single woman, but at the age of forty with much of her life behind her. Although I interviewed other unattached women of her age in France, Virginia's story demonstrates better than any the countless ways in which emigration can touch the life of a Portuguese woman.

Ana is from the city of Porto and from a working-class family.

While the majority of Portuguese migrants in France are of rural backgrounds, I felt that it was important to show the way in which an urban family has become involved in emigration and to contrast the experiences of an urban working-class woman with those of rural peasant women. Ana also differs in that she was married prior to her emigration and her decision to leave Portugal was largely determined by that of her husband. The majority of married Portuguese women in France emigrated to join their spouses abroad. However, Ana's story illustrates a pattern of migration common among only some of these women—they emigrate without their children, hoping that within three years or so they will be able to return to Portugal for good. Theirs is a reluctant emigration.

In physical appearance, Ricardina, Virginia, and Ana are very much alike and are typical of the Portuguese *mulher forte*, the short, stocky, robust woman. In personality, however, they are quite different, and these differences emerge clearly in their story telling. Ricardina is the most temperamental of the three: impulsive, ambitious, and not unlike many other young single women I interviewed who had emigrated in search of a life better than that of the Portuguese *mulher do campo* ("peasant woman"). Her ambition may derive from a relatively isolated and unprosperous social background from which emigration provides the only definite escape. Virginia, despite her ten-year seniority over Ricardina and Ana, is the gayest, and expresses the most curiosity about the people and things around her. Like her Minhotan compatriots, she comes alive at a festa and displays a generosity and warmth that have long been considered characteristic of the people of northwestern Portugal. Virginia's ability to face the world alone is rather remarkable, but again not uncharacteristic of the courage of Portuguese peasant women in general. Ana is the most serious of the three, with a somewhat fatalistic streak. Her urban origins, and particularly the relative absence of a network of familial or communal support in France, may account for this seriousness. Although all three women were constantly making plans and thinking about the future, Ana worried the most, a result, perhaps, of the rather unsettling circumstances of living with her husband, but apart from her children.

In choosing these three narratives to represent the varying patterns of migration for Portuguese women, there is one major omission: married women who migrate with their children to join husbands who have been abroad for several years. Although I did interview a few such women, I was not able to assemble from any of them a narrative as detailed as those given to me by other women who were, perhaps, more personally involved in a migration decision. However, some of the experiences that these women face are addressed by Ricardina and Virginia in references they make to their sisters.

II. COLLECTING AND ASSEMBLING THE STORIES

Many anthropologists who write or talk about the process of collecting life histories from so-called "ordinary" people refer frequently to a "who me?" syndrome. Informants sometimes wonder why the anthropologist is so interested in their personal life. After all, they do not consider it to be special so why should anyone else! I was greeted, however, with quite a different response by almost all the women I interviewed who, at one point or another during our acquaintance commented, "Senhora, a minha vida é um romance" ("my life is a novel"). Virginia, Ricardina, and Ana were no exception. They each felt that they had something to say and were quite willing to recount it to me. They had, to use Kelley's phrase, a "sense of self." Kelley relates the openness of her own informants, and their ready acceptance of the life history method, to aspects of Yaqui culture and society. A similar assessment could be made with reference to the Portuguese, whose most national style of music, the fado, is essentially a melancholic story telling. Indeed, the choice of the word "romance" itself implies a balladlike tale that contains a certain element of drama. In addition, various scholars of Portugal have, on occasion, made passing reference to individuality and independence as essential aspects of the Portuguese character, aspects associated perhaps most closely with the emigratory spirit.

When I approached Ricardina, Ana, and Virginia, I told them that I was writing a book about Portuguese women in France. The fact that I spoke Portuguese fluently and that I had come all the way from the United States to talk to them (that is, I was not French) somehow helped to establish rapport. All three stories were collected between September 1974 and June 1975. I met Ana and Virginia earlier, and repeated visits with them over an extended period of time changed my role quickly from one of unknown investigator to one of close friend and confidante.

Ana was initially introduced to me through a cultural center which provides social services and general aid to immigrants in France. It was late August and she had just returned from a month's vacation in Portugal. She came to the center with her husband to say hello to the director, a French woman, and complained that every time she went to Portugal she put on weight. After our first meeting at the center, I visited Ana at her home in the Parisian suburb of Eaubonne several more times over the course of a year. I talked to her alone on afternoons when she worked the morning shift at the clinic where she was employed. On each visit she reported her latest plans, ailments, triumphs or annoyances.

Of the three women, Ana was the most comfortable using French, and she frequently switched back and forth between two languages during our conversations. When she was talking about events in her own life, she would often act them out, changing her voice and expression to suit the character she was portraying and making me the other player in the reenactment. On occasions, she even let a common French expletive slip in, but quickly begged my pardon. At the end of each afternoon I spent with her, she, like all the other Portuguese women who welcomed me into their homes and into their lives, prepared tea, and our conversation turned to mundane domestic matters: how she wanted to rearrange a room, what furniture she wanted to buy. On these occasions, she would often ask me about myself and sometimes even offer advice as one friend to another and as one woman to another.

I met Virginia Caldas midway through my year in France at a Sunday morning mass for Portuguese immigrants in the parish of St. Jean Baptiste, Neuilly. The young Portuguese priest introduced me to her and I was struck immediately by her warmth and full-of-life quality. She began to tell me about a recent operation that had kept her from her work for the previous month and extended an invitation for me to visit her during the following week on her afternoon off. We met that time and on several subsequent Thursday afternoons in her little room on the first floor of the modern apartment building where she worked as a maid for a French family. The room was simply furnished with a bed, dresser, desk, chair, and cabinet where she kept Port wine and biscuits. Over her bed was a wooden cross and a rosary and on one wall there was a poster of Princess Anne—about whom she commented "she has not had a baby yet" (this was February 1975). Virginia began to talk about herself with the phrase that opens her story, "my life is no secret."

She shared her thoughts and feelings with me as openly as that phrase implies and a friendship developed between us that has lasted to the present.

During the summer of 1975, I spent time with Virginia in her native village in Portugal and was able to meet many members of her family. This gave me a unique opportunity to confirm many aspects of her story and to gain a greater understanding of her background than that gained by a portrait at a distance.

I met Ricardina during the last month of my stay in France at a small fête for Portuguese immigrants in the eighth arrondissement of Paris. She was at the party with her brother and sister-in-law whom I had met previously. Of all the women I interviewed over the course of a year, Ricardina was the most suspicious and wanted to know exactly how I came to be doing the research and who paid for it. However, she was also intrigued with the idea of telling me her life story. Since she held a position as a concierge and was at home most of the day, we were able to work intensively on the story for three weeks. Indeed, only in Ricardina's case was a life story, in a truer sense of the method, collected, and for this reason her narrative is the least fragmented of the three. Her account was more self-generated and self-motivated and is, therefore, more easily compared to documents such as Carolina de Jesus' diary or Washburne's life story of the Eskimo woman Anauta.[5]

Although Ricardina did not return to Portugal herself during the summer of 1975, I was able to visit her village and chatted briefly with members of her family. One of her uncles showed me through the house that she and her husband had purchased in the village with money earned in France and pointed out other places that she had mentioned in our discussions. This visit made it easier for me to comprehend the dramatic move across space, and even time, that Ricardina had made in emigrating to France.

Despite the slightly different circumstances under which each of the stories was collected, I approached the task in a similar fashion. I began the first interview session by having the women tell me how they came to France. Each of them told her story differently: Ricardina and Virginia placed more emphasis on the reasons for their departure, while Ana gave much more attention to her first years of life in France. On subsequent visits, aspects of their stories were clarified and filled out and slowly the subjects of conversation expanded to include more details of their lives prior to emigration.

It was only through this process of clarification, for example, that Ricardina began to tell me about the events surrounding her marriage and the birth of her first child.

The questions I raised were very broad and based largely on something that had been said in a previous session. We normally started with these questions, but if the conversation turned in other directions, I let it turn. One day, for example, Ana greeted me with a letter in hand that she had received from her eldest daughter. She told me that her daughter had written that she never wanted to come to France. This led immediately into a discussion of the agony that Ana felt in being a "mother at a distance."

The stories and descriptions of village life and the accounts of particular events in their lives as migrants are things that Ana, Ricardina, and Virginia chose to relate—things which they felt to be most salient. It is largely in this sense—in the choice of subject matter— that the "presentation of self" emerges most clearly. However, while all three narratives are personal accounts by three quite different women, each of these women is, at times, able to be objective and reflective and to make statements that are part of a public culture that they all share as Portuguese women or as Portuguese migrant women. They all comment, for example, about what emigration has meant for Portugal as a whole. Their acquaintance with the French way of life allows them to be comparative in discussions of particular customs and values.

Since two of the three narratives were collected more as a series of ethnographic interviews or conversations rather than as more formal life histories, a great deal of thought was put into precisely how they were to be assembled and presented. Obviously, a certain amount of editing was necessary to delete repetitions and to organize the data into a more coherent story. In Ricardina's case, some of the material in the Portuguese edition of her story (see note 5) was omitted here in order to make her account roughly equal in length to the other two and to permit me to analyze systematically the three stories as a single unit as well as separately. Purist proponents of the life-history method will, perhaps, object to this and I can only ask them tó trust my judgment regarding material excluded from the present version and refer them to the Portuguese edition for the more complete and largely unedited version.

One major decision was to organize the narratives into chronological order. While this is not necessarily the most natural way in which an individual recalls his or her own life (even Ricardina moved back and forth in time), it does make it easier to follow and to comprehend the series of circumstances that led each of the three women to the decision to emigrate. It also facilitates drawing comparisons between their varied experiences. A second decision was to present the stories in the first person in an attempt to remain as faithful as possible to the women's own accounts and to convey a sense of their individual personalities. I have tried to maintain the impression of their spoken language, using phrases they used and the short expressive sentences that are so much a part of conversational autobiography. This includes the occasional quoting of the songs and dictums that are often cited by the Portuguese to explain complicated ideas or sentiments.

I have restricted my own analytical comments to the introduction of each narrative and to the conclusion. In addition, chapter one provides a general background to the role of women in Portuguese emigration and treats briefly the legal, religious, and structural definitions of women's status in Portuguese society. The material contained in this chapter should help the reader to grasp more fully the political-economic context that made it possible for Ricardina, Ana, and Virginia to migrate to France. In addition, it provides a basis for understanding some of the cultural implications or foundations of particular statements made by the three women and to distinguish these from aspects of their lives that might be considered more idiosyncratic. By maintaining a first person narrative style and by distinctly separating my remarks from the ethnographic text, it is possible to differentiate between the meanings which each of the women personally ascribes to her own life as a Portuguese woman and as a migrant woman from the meanings that I ascribe to their lives collectively as an outside interpreter. In addition, it leaves the stories open to interpretations other than those that I give them.

I would like to conclude these introductory remarks with a brief comment about the question of anonymity. After much soul-searching and subsequent discussions with the three women themselves, I have decided to use their own names and the photographs that they permitted me to take to include in the book. In recent years, a few anthropologists have addressed the issue of pseudonyms in the reporting of anthropological data.[6] The aim, and I think it is still a valid one, is to protect informants from any repercussions, foreseen or unforeseen, which might occur upon publication of the research. In some cases, researchers have also altered some of the essential data in order to disguise more fully a place or a group of people. In other cases, they have taken their manuscripts back to their community or to their informants. However, as Barnes has wisely noted, "the dividing line between fact and interpretation is (in this case) usually problematic, and citizens may be just as keen to point out errors of interpretation, as they see it, as errors of fact. It is hard to draw a clear line between a proper respect for a citizen's right to privacy and excessive respect for the accuracy of his interpretation of events."[7]

The stories presented here were collected with the informed consent of the three women involved and they are published under the same conditions, although none of the women has seen the final manuscript. In recontacting the women five years after first amassing the material, I found that each of them was able to recall quite vividly what she had told me and they they were all fully at ease with the fact that strangers would soon read what they had recounted. However, while the personal names are accurate, the anonymity of the two villages concerned has been retained. This was my own decision, taken to protect the privacy of family members or other individuals who are essentially unaware of what has been said about them and to remain consistent with other publications where I have used a pseudonym for Virginia's village in particular.

CHAPTER ONE

Portugal, Emigration, and the Status of Women: A Background

Although this book concentrates upon the individual migrant, it is important to consider the cultural-historical tradition within which emigration is an option. The first part of this chapter is therefore devoted to a brief examination of the history of emigration within Portuguese society and a more complete analysis of contemporary Portuguese migration to France. The role played by Portuguese women in these movements of population—both historically and at present—is emphasized. The political-economic "reality" of certain factors such as employment opportunities, immigration policy, and the character of urban life serve as a backdrop against which the personal "reality" of the individual stories can be set.

The second part of the chapter points to specific structural features that have been important definers of the status of women in Salazarist Portugal. The three women whose stories are presented in this book were raised under a regime where patriarchal attitudes were reinforced by civil and administrative codes and where economic and social mobility within Portugal—for lower-class women in particular—was thwarted not only by these codes, but also by an ossified social system that sharply divided rich and poor. While none of them referred either consciously or specifically to the impact of Portuguese laws, the Church, or social hierarchy upon their lives, it is clear that these factors have shaped their lives and those of all other Portuguese women born and raised during Salazar's *Estado Novo*. Again, this helps to provide a transition from a discussion of experiences that are common or collective to a discussion of the way in which these collective experiences are played out in the lives and perceptions of particular individuals.

I. PORTUGAL: AN EMIGRATING SOCIETY

> The idea to emigrate resides in the breast of each man. . . . It comes
> from his great grandfathers, from further still. . . . All generations
> are born with this innate aspiration and it makes a nuisance of itself
> when it is not satisfied. It always lurks around a corner in the mind
> to be brought out as a talisman in moments of challenge to fate, or
> used as a prop in times when desperate remedies are needed.[1]

With these words, the Portuguese novelist Ferreira de Castro has
encapsulated the emigratory spirit of his compatriots. Since the fif-
teenth century and the age of Henry the Navigator, Portuguese
nationals have turned their spyglasses westward and southward
across the waters of the Atlantic in search of new lands and new
riches. Throughout this first century of expansion, Portuguese ships
explored the western coasts of the African continent. At the close
of the century, the voyages of Vasco da Gama expanded the hori-
zons of Portuguese traders and adventurers and, during the following two centuries, Portuguese people firmly installed themselves on
the shores of India and Asia. According to Charles Boxer, a noted
historian of the Portuguese empire, the organization and planning
of these voyages was due in large part to "intelligent government
initiative and support."

> The Portuguese empire in Asia and Africa can be described as a
> commercial and maritime empire cast in a military and ecclesiastical
> mold. Every male Portuguese who went to the *Estado da India* did so
> in the service of the Crown or of the Church.[2]

The specific use of the word *male* is significant for throughout this
period few women left Portugal, whether to Asia or Africa. The
only women who did emigrate with the approval of the crown were
the so-called "Orphans of the King," the Portuguese counterpart to
the *Filles de Roi* of French overseas expansion. These young women
were furnished, according to Boxer, with dowries in the form
of minor government posts offered to any man who would marry
them. Their numbers were small and their mortality rate high.
Thus most men who had ventured to imperial shores were left
to enter into miscegenous unions—legal or illicit—with native
women.[3]

Although the Portuguese were also exploring the coastline of the

American continent during the sixteenth and seventeenth centuries, it was the discovery of gold and diamonds in the Brazilian heartland in the eighteenth century that inaugurated the period of Brazilian dominance in Portuguese overseas expansion. In the view of Portuguese historian Joel Serrão, it was with this phase of exploration and settlement that the Portuguese emigrant *strictu sensu* came into being. Unlike the *colono* of earlier centuries, the eighteenth-century emigrant to Brazil left his homeland on his own initiative rather than through state initiative.

By 1770, the population of "foreigners" in Brazil had risen to one and one-half million from a figure of roughly 150,000 at the end of sixteenth century, largely as a result of emigration from continental Portugal. This emigration included individuals from the literate and propertied (*fidalgo*) classes of Portuguese society, who went to Brazil invested with official administrative functions, as well as individuals from the poorer, more illiterate sectors of Portuguese society. The majority of these poorer emigrants became part of the mercantile class in Brazil, establishing themselves as commercial shopkeepers and small-time artisans. Their ambition, as Serrão notes, was to enrich themselves through lucrative business ventures. They chose to remain in Brazil, adopting it as their new homeland. Although historians acknowledge the greater volume of female migration to Brazil in comparison with that to Africa and the East, they still refer to colonial Brazil as a male-dominated society where mixed marriages were frequent.

Emigration to the Brazilian colony reached such proportions that new laws were passed by the latter part of the eighteenth century in an attempt to counteract the rapid augmentation in the rate of outflow and to halt the dramatic depletion of population in certain regions of the country. Emigration came to be restricted to those who left for specific administrative and religious tasks in the colonies. Only in the late nineteenth century did a resurgence occur— a resurgence which involved the rural and urban poor of Portugal in emigration to a much greater extent than in any previous period.

Impetus for this new wave of emigration to Brazil came in 1888 in the aftermath of the abolition of slavery. Manpower was needed to do the work that had been done by black slaves prior to 1888 on the large Brazilian fazendas. Immigrants from Portugal could no longer hope to establish themselves in small businesses. Rather, they became field hands.

They sleep, eat and work like slaves. They have their ration of dried meat, beans and flour which they have to cook for lunch and dinner. Their slave quarters consist of small unfloored rooms with a door and a window, a mat for a bed and a stone to sit on. They work like slaves, commanded by a foreman, beginning at dawn and ending at nine at night.[4]

This turn-of-the-century Portuguese emigration was *predominated* by poor peasants, especially from northern Portugal—a feature explained not only by the need for agricultural manpower in Brazil, but also by several other factors: the growth in population in the northern Portuguese countryside in the latter part of the nineteenth century, the phyloxera disaster of the 1870s that destroyed most of the vineyards in the northern viticultural regions, the expansion of the railroad, and the increasingly burdensome taxes that were imposed upon the Portuguese populace during an economically crisis-ridden century. Between 1888 and 1924, the annual rate of emigration from Portugal was about fifteen thousand, attaining maximum rates in the years just prior to the First World War. Although the majority of these emigrants went to Brazil, there was also an important flow of manpower to Spain in the 1870s and 1880s, and again after the First World War during the decade of the 1920s.

TABLE 1
Percentages of Men and Women among Portuguese Emigrants, 1868–1960

Year (by period)	Men (%)	Women (%)
1868–1877	92	8
1878–1890	88	12
1891–1900	78	22
1901–1911	80	20
1912–1920	70	30
1921–1930	78	22
1931–1940	65	35
1941–1950	65	35
1951–1960	60	40

Source: Serrao (1974), Figure 5, p. 124.

The traditional pattern of emigration for the rural peasantry closely paralleled that of their social superiors. Single men and male heads of households emigrated leaving their women and children in the villages to continue to work the small plots of land that families owned or rented.[5] These women waited patiently from month to month and year to year for the men to return. Some did return, with or without small fortunes. Others were swallowed by the booming cities of Brazil, never to be seen or heard from again. As a result, many Portuguese peasant wives dressed themselves in black on the day their husbands departed and came to be known, especially in the northwestern province of Minho, which has had consistently high rates of emigration, as *viuvas dos vivos* ("widows of the living"). Popular poetry abounds with references to these apprehensive and waiting women.

> *Tenho o peito fechado*
> *A chave está em Brazil*
> *O meu peito não se abre*
> *Sem a chave de là vir*

> "My breast is closed
> The key is in Brazil
> My breast will not open
> Until the key returns from there"

Indeed, the tradition of male emigration has probably been the most significant factor defining the economic role of women in northern Portugal, a role which numerous travelers to the region have remarked on.

> Such are the normal duties of women here. For the men of the district, possessed with an unconquerable aversion for this form of labor, are well content to leave the soil of their wives and daughters while they, for their part, go out into the world and adopt the less strenuous callings of carpenters, masons, and waiters.[6]

A division of labor which has persisted into the present, especially in the province of Minho, was firmly established. Not even the most arduous tasks are left to men as they are in other peasant societies. Portuguese women prepare, till, and irrigate the fields, and participate in all forms of harvesting. They are as handy as the men with a pitchfork, piling up haystacks or loading ox carts with the mountain underbrush used in the stables to make fertilizer. Around the house they care for the oxen and farm animals, milk the cows, and fatten the pigs. They carry formidable loads on their heads wherever they go, a practice that has given them a characteristic gait. In addition to their agricultural chores, they perform all the necessary domestic activities that their husbands, if present, are never expected to perform since this would earn them the title *marica*, the derogatory Portuguese term for an effeminate male. Domestic activities do not simply involve cooking, housecleaning, and childcare. Until manufactured fabrics became more readily available in the 1950s, women were responsible for the cultivation and home manufacture of linen for clothing and household use. This was an activity that kept them busy throughout the winter months when agricultural chores were less demanding.

Some writers have pointed to the importance of women in the economy of rural Portugal as an indication of the "matriarchal" character of that way of life. However, it is also possible to suggest that the division of labor that essentially left much of the agricultural work to women was a means by which Portuguese peasant men maintained a position of dominance over women. Within the social hierarchy of occupations, work in the fields, which dirties your hands, is more degrading that the cleaner occupations of skilled craftsmen. One noted scholar of Portuguese society has made exactly this observation.

> [The women] work regularly in the fields and even in the quarries, and they row heavy barges . . . The position of women in Portugal is another instance of vague ideals. Woman is set on a pedestal, but women are not always treated with consideration and in some parts of the country are little better than slaves. Over and over again you will meet a man and a woman, husband and wife perhaps, the man in lordly fashion carrying a small parcel or nothing at all, the woman bowing under a huge load . . . The peasant women continue to do twice the labor of men and to receive half the wages.[7]

A peasant woman reiterated this assessment even more succinctly: "The men want to be *fidalgos*. They are too proud (*vaidoso*) to work in the fields. The life of a Portuguese woman is a slave's life (*uma vida escrava*)."

Although Brazil remained the major destination of the majority of Portuguese emigrants in the immediate post-World War II period, this privileged position began to erode after 1958 with the increasing flow of Portuguese migrant workers to northern Europe. In recent years, much has been written about this new and quite dramatic population movement,[8] a movement based essentially upon the same mutual interaction of needs between sending and receiving societies that had characterized earlier phases of Portuguese emigration: the need of the developed countries of northern Europe for workers to fill the posts that their own countrymen would no longer fill, and the need of the underdeveloped countries of southern Europe to export their surplus population. The capitalistic enterprises of France, Germany, Switzerland, and Belgium turned to rely on a reserve army of foreign workers who would satisfy the demands for cheap labor, increased production, and the desire for expanding profits without further augmentation of salaries or alterations in working conditions. Immigrant workers would accept lower salaries, longer and irregular working hours, dangerous jobs, and substandard living conditions. The less developed countries of Italy, Spain, Portugal, Greece, Turkey, and even Yugoslavia, saw this new intra-European movement, especially if it was carried out on a temporary or semipermanent basis, as a means of bringing new wealth into their countries and of obtaining "free" vocational training for their semiskilled and unskilled labor force.[9]

In the last fifteen to twenty years, some ten million workers have made the great trek northward to the more industrialized countries of northwestern Europe, to build their buildings, clean their streets, houses, and hotel rooms, and to advance their manufacturing industries. According to statistics of the French minister of labor, the total foreign worker population in France in 1975 numbered roughly four million; that is, approximately 7.7 percent of the total population of France and approximately 8.5 percent of the total active population. In Switzerland, foreign workers came to compose over 30 percent of the active labor force, a factor which began to worry the native Swiss population and which culminated in the early 1970s in a referendum proposed by the ultraconservative National Action party. If this referendum had passed, it would have resulted in the deportation of approximately one-half million foreign workers over a three-year period.

In the mid 1960s, 71 percent of all foreign workers in France were from the Iberian peninsula and at present the Portuguese are still

TABLE 2
Portuguese Immigration to France 1946–1975 (legal)

Year	Permanent Workers[a]	Seasonal Laborers[b]	Familial Immigration[c]
1946	-------	-------	-------
1947	-------	-------	-------
1948	-------	-------	-------
1949	-------	-------	86
1950	72	-------	242
1951	260	-------	158
1952	472	-------	178
1953	438	-------	252
1954	459	-------	288
1955	949	-------	387
1956	1,432	-------	419
1957	4,160	-------	480
1958	5,054	-------	1,210
1959	3,339	126	1,499
1960	4,007	937	2,427
1961	6,716	1,328	3,776
1962	12,916	1,368	3,882
1963	24,781	2,269	5,062
1964	43,751	3,729	7,917
1965	47,330	4,190	12,937
1966	44,916	3,035	18,695
1967	34,764	3,131	24,833
1968	30,868	3,110	27,873
1969	80,829	3,063	29,785
1970	88,634	3,004	47,033
1971	64,328	2,821	46,492
1972	30,475	2,837	38,217
1973	32,082	2,674	31,861
1974	14,329	2,094	23,398
1975	4,946	2,138	18,490
Total	582,307	41,859	347,877

a. Permanent workers include those issued work and residence permits.
b. Seasonal workers are those issued a temporary permit, normally for nine months.
c. Familial immigration includes women and children who enter France under the title of familial immigration rather than that of permanent worker.

Source: Office National d'Immigration, Statistiques de l'Immigration 1975.

one of the largest foreign groups. In 1950, 314 Portuguese immigrants entered France, but by 1970, the peak year for Portuguese immigration, the figure had reached 110,615 (Table 2). Portuguese emigration during the decade of the 1960s represented a 2 percent loss in population per year, leading ex-premier Marcello Caetano to term it a "bloodletting" more massive than at any other period in the country's history.

After 1971, the annual rates of Portuguese emigration to France declined; first, as a result of an agreement signed between Portugal and France limiting the entrance of Portuguese workers to 65,000 per year, and second, as a result of worldwide problems of inflation and unemployment after 1974 which dried up the market for immigrant labor.

Although the rapid increase in Portuguese emigration after 1958 is explained largely by the "pull factors" of the post-World War II industrial boom in northern Europe, a perpetuation of both local and national economic and demographic problems within Portugal itself continued to provide an impetus for population movement. Portuguese policy makers viewed this recent phase of emigration as a source of stimulation for the Portuguese economy and as a means of solving a massive unemployment and underemployment problem.

A few details about the Portuguese economy at the beginning of the last decade help to clarify the benefits that emigration could yield. In 1970, the gross national product per capita of the country was $640 (compared with $1,150 for Spain, $2,290 for France and $4,480 for the United States). The rate of industrialization was still low and regionally concentrated. Close to 30 percent of the population was still employed in the agricultural sector, 35 percent in industry, and 31 percent in services. This can be compared to 25 percent in agriculture, 37 percent in industry, and 37 percent in services in Spain; 14 percent in agriculture, 35 percent in industry, and 40 percent in services in France; 4 percent in agriculture, 32 percent in industry, and 60 percent in services in the United States. The colonial wars in Africa consumed 40 percent of the national budget between 1970 and 1975. Funds were therefore short for the development of the productive sector and the initiation of needed programs of education and social welfare.

Emigration to France brought new wealth into the country through emigrant remittances. By the early 1970s, remittances had reached roughly $200 million per year (Table 3). This provided foreign exchange to match one-third of the import bill and made a significant contribution to alleviate the serious trade deficit that Portugal had accumulated.

TABLE 3
Remittances of Portuguese Emigrants, 1950–1970
(in 1000 of contos: 1 conto = approx. $40 in 1975)

Year	Remittances[a]
1950	504
1954	320
1958	1,552
1962	1,704
1963	2,371
1964	2,679
1965	3,378
1966	4,818
1967	6,267
1968	7,902
1969	11,812
1970	14,343

a. Until 1955 the transferences of emigrants only; after 1956, gifts, bequests, and pensions also included.

Source: Sousa Ferreira (1976), Quadro 28, p. 131.

Despite these obvious advantages, emigration was only "approved of" within certain limits, a factor which in large part explains one of the most characteristic features of Portuguese emigration to France: illegal or clandestine emigration. Although clandestine departure has always played a role in Portuguese emigration, its volume has never been quite as dramatic as during the decade of the 1960s. The origins of this massive illegal outflow can be found in the escalation of the colonial wars in Portuguese Africa after 1961. Many young men simply chose emigration over military service. In addition, a rigid set of regulations was created to limit the legal emigration of young men who wished to leave Portugal *before* reaching the official age (eighteen) for military conscription.

The Portuguese government also began to fear the political climate to which emigrants might be exposed abroad, especially in a country like France where national workers' unions thrive. Stiff regulations specified the following requirements before a passport for legal emigration was issued: employment in the country of destination guaranteed, support of the family that remained in Portugal assured, military obligations fulfilled, paternal consent where necessary, and a minimum degree of education (four years of schooling). In addition, certain quotas were established for each region of Portugal so as not to deplete the working population too drastically. The rigidity of these laws and the time that it took to secure a passport steered more and more potential emigrants of all ages in the direction of illegal or clandestine departure.

The clandestine Portuguese emigrant frequently paid a *passador* ("guide") anywhere from four to eight contos ($80-320) to lead him across the Portuguese frontier into Spain and often through Spain into France. Almost every Portuguese immigrant one meets in France has a story of *o salto* ("the leap")—his or her own voyage, or that of a close relative, on foot, in a refrigerated truck, or in the trunk of a car. Once in France, it was imperative to obtain the *carte de sejour* and the *carte de travail*, the two documents necessary to remain and work legally in France. Frequently, a Portuguese immigrant worked for several months before legalizing his position and as an illegal alien was often subject to all forms of exploitation. The problems of clandestine emigration became so grave that several decrees were issued by the French in late 1960s in an attempt to alleviate the situation. In December 1968, all those who had arrived illegally to that date were legalized. In November 1969, a decree was formulated which made clandestine emigration a petty offence subject to a small fine; finally, in July 1970, another decree made it possible to pay the fine and obtain a passport in one of the Portuguese consular offices in France.

It was largely the formidable surge in Portuguese immigration, legal and illegal, together with the immigration of North Africans, that caused the crisis of the *bidonvilles*, which exploded into French consciousness in the mid 1960s. The term comes from the French word *bidons*, "oil cans," which are hammered flat to provide construction materials. These bidonvilles sprung up on unprepared land surrounding the major cities of France near construction sites where foreign workers were employed, or on old construction sites where scrap materials were available. In the early 1960s, approximately twelve thousand Portuguese resided in the bidonville of Champigny to the east of Paris. Most of the early immigrants in France spent a year or more in these places. Others, if they did not live in one of the numerouse bidonvilles, live on the *chantier*, the temporary housing set up by many of the construction firms on the building sites. They moved with the company when the current building project terminated.

These living arrangements were a result of the predominantly male composition of the immigrant population which was in turn a consequence of immigration policies that suited the momentary needs of economic expansion. These male foreigners were a temporary labor force and, as in the late nineteenth century, the villages of northern Portugal (like villages elsewhere in the Mediterranean region) became largely populated by women and children: the wives, sons, and daughters of *os franceses*, the Portuguese migrant workers in France.[10]

However, beginning in 1965 and especially after 1968, increasing numbers of Portuguese women have also emigrated to France. The increase in female emigration came with a dramatic shift in France's immigration policy, a shift which did not explicitly occur, for example, in the immigration policies of some other northern European countries.[11] Nineteen sixty-eight marked a return to the natalist propaganda of the post-World War II Gaulist era and its effect on immigration policy has been manifested in the new emphasis on the regrouping of entire families abroad. As Minces has noted:

> Among migrants there are proportionally more adults of working age than among the French. It is precisely because their demographic dynamism is high that the French government aims at settling them more permanently in France, facilitating procedures for naturalization and the introduction of families . . . A strong state is a peopled state. Immigration represented one third of the total demographic growth between 1969 and 1971 and approximately 12% of the annual births are of foreign parents.[12]

Jumping dramatically in the latter 1960s and early 1970s, the proportion of Portuguese immigrant women in France is high when compared with other immigrant groups (Table 4). Among married women entering France in the latter 1960s, the majority came to join their husbands. Among single women, as many came independently in search of work as came as part of the new familial migration process.

TABLE 4
Female Immigrants as a Percentage of Total Immigrants by Nationality, 1968 and 1973

Nationality	1968	1973
Spanish	28.2%	21.8%
Italian	25.3%	20.3%
Portuguese	9.1%	21.2%
Polish	8.5%	5.2%
Yugoslav	2.0%	2.5%
Algerian	7.2%	8.2%
Tunisian	1.8%	2.5%
Moroccan	1.4%	2.9%
Others	16.5%	2.5%

Source: Wisniewski (1974); based on 1968 national census data and figures issued by the minister of the interior 1/1/1973

One of the most distinctive factors about Portuguese immigrant women in France is their high level of employment. Even women who emigrate with their children primarily to join their husbands soon move out into the labor force. Close to 50 percent of Portuguese women above age fifteen are actively employed, working on an average more hours per week than women of other foreign nationalities in France. Until the mid 1970s, the majority of these women were employed in the private domestic sector as full-time maids (*bonnes à toute faire*), cleaning ladies (*femmes de ménage*), or as porters (*concièrges*). In the mid 1970s, a gradual shift occurred toward greater employment in the secondary sector (Table 5). According to the way in which these figures are compiled, some of this shift can be accounted for by a move from employment in the private domestic sector to what might be considered a public domestic sector—the employment of Portuguese women by cleaning firms or by the cleaning staff of various public institutions such as hospitals. On the whole, it has been difficult for Portuguese

TABLE 5
Evolution of the Active Female Population by Nationality in Major Occupational Sectors, 1968–1975

	Service Personnel				Factory or Large Company Employees				Office Workers			
	1968	%	1975	%	1968	%	1975	%	1968	%	1975	%
Spanish	37,740	53	25,595	44	21,320	30	20,665	35	3,644	5	6,030	20
Portuguese	11,260	43	33,335	30	12,244	47	64,485	59	752	3	6,350	6
Algerian	1,048	16	2,700	15	3,500	56	9,060	52	912	14	4,360	25
Moroccan	780	27	2,835	29	828	28	4,630	48	884	30	1,230	12
Tunisian	440	11	1,055	13	1,332	34	2,745	46	1,744	44	1,540	30

Source: Institut National de la Statistique et des Études Économiques (INSEE), France

women to break into factory work, an area of activity reserved in large part for the French female labor force.

For Portuguese women in France, gainful employment does not necessarily represent a distinct departure from a traditional way of life as it might for women of other foreign immigrant groups. Many peasant girls had previously worked in domestic service in Portugal, in the textile factories in the north or in agriculture as hired day-laborers (*jornaleiras*). Women with this kind of previous work experience have fewer problems adapting than those who were primarily self-employed on their own lands. However, even for rural peasant women the adaptations are qualitative rather than quantitative. Having to work for others rather than simply for themselves is one aspect of this difference; another is the steadiness of the work, its hourly routine, and its independence from the seasonal variations in climate which are so important in farm life; a third is the shift from an economy that is largely subsistence-oriented to one that is more consumer-oriented.

The first job is usually found with the help of compatriots already well settled in France, most often a relative or fellow villager. Once a woman has become more adept at life in France, job mobility occurs as she seeks out a position most suited to her personal and familial needs. Single women, young or old, who have emigrated alone, prefer positions as full-time maids which provide them not only with economic security, but also with housing security. Women who have migrated with their husbands and left their children behind prefer cleaning lady positions with hourly wages which allow them the freedom to work as much as fourteen hours a day. Their major goal is to earn as much as possible. Young mothers prefer concierge positions which allow them to combine the responsibilities of child-care with some economic contribution to the support of the family. However, these different forms of domestic service are not necessarily mutually exclusive. Concierges, for example, depending on the age of their children or the particular obligations associated with their concierge position (something which does vary from one part of the city to the next), often supplement their janitorial duties with hours of cleaning within the neighborhood. Others clean public buildings in the evenings when their husbands are home with the children.

Except for work in public buildings which can involve a group of women working together, most Portuguese women employed in domestic service work in isolation from their compatriots and comment upon this as a change from work in the fields where you can stop to chat with other workers or with people passing by. However, they are by no means as isolated as those women who do not work at all in France and who consequently have little oppor-tunity to learn French. These latter women, most often women with larger families, are perhaps the least adapted to life in France.

Working Portuguese women generally view their employment as a positive change from agricultural labor which is dirtier, less regular, and less secure (in the sense of being more dependent upon the frivolities of nature). The adjustments that they must make to their work are perhaps less difficult than those that their husbands must make because domestic tasks are very familiar to them. They usually only have to learn to use vacuum cleaners and other machines of modern housekeeping and, if they cook, to prepare particular French dishes. Portuguese men, on the other hand, must acquire new skills appropriate, for example, to large-scale construc-tion or automobile assembly.

While employment does not represent a dramatic departure from the traditional way of life for Portuguese migrant women in France, changes in domestic relations for married women are significant and viewed generally as "for the better." There is greater sharing of both household responsibilities and leisure time. Portuguese men in France often do the shopping, occasional cooking and cleaning, and other small domestic tasks that they would not perform in Portugal. They alter their behavior in France not only because of the economic constraints of being part of a migrant family, but also because French men help their wives with domestic chores. When they return to Portugal for the summer, however, many revert to the expected roles of their own country. They do not carry parcels, work in the kitchen, or sit with their wives in church as they do in France.

Not only do Portuguese immigrant couples in France share do-mestic duties, they also spend more leisure time together, a definite change from Portugal where the spheres for leisure time activities are frequently distinctly separate. This separation is most succinctly expressed in the adage O homem na praça; a mulher em casa ("The man in the square and the woman in the house"). In France, the public sphere of the praça or the café is often lacking and consequently

Portuguese men remain at home with their wives and children watching television, discussing their plans for the future, or generally relaxing. Most major decisions are made together at this time.

Although the first major problem that all Portuguese migrants must resolve is that of language, the differences they see in coming to France beyond that are primarily those between a rural environment and an urban environment. Both men and women weigh these differences carefully, but generally the contrast is between the city as the best place to work and earn a living and the country as the best place to live. In the city, "everything is convenient; it is easier to buy the things you want; you earn more and eat better," but "people are nervous and the noise gives you headaches." In the country, on the other hand, "the air is pure and healthier and people are more friendly." These are the most typical assessments.

Despite the favorable evaluation of village friendliness, however, there are many Portuguese migrant women who express a definite preference for the anonymity and privacy of urban living. They do not have to account for their activities. They can live as they like and do what they like without everyone else knowing about it or talking about it. In this sense, Portuguese women, both single and married, appreciate the independence or "freedom" that life in France has given them.

The migration of women and children is the first step, for most families, toward a permanent settlement in France. One might say that the initial strategy of migration, where the man was expected to spend three to six years in France and then return for good, has changed. However, permanent settlement in France does not mean that Portuguese immigrants, both male and female, completely abandon their attachment to their homeland and their hopes of returning there some day. Indeed, most Portuguese immigrants return to Portugal each summer to *matar as saudades* ("quell their nostalgia"). During the last weekend in July and the first weekend in August, cars owned by *os franceses* clog the major border points between Spain and Portugal. The villages of the north come alive for a month as emigrants join their compatriots in the celebration of the annual local festas. While some spend their time putting new touches on the houses they have built with their hard-earned French francs, others simply return to relax and remember.

II. THE LAW, THE CHURCH AND THE BOURGEOISIE: DEFINERS OF WOMEN'S STATUS IN SALAZARIST PORTUGAL

> Certain doors in social life were closed for me when I was still a student. When they reopened, I was of retirement age. How many times have I repeated to myself this paraphrase of Rostand: "Liberty, I have searched for you from dawn without finding you; now I find you and it is already night.[13]

With this words, Dr. Elina Guimarães, a renowned Portuguese jurist who wrote on matters pertaining to Portuguese women throughout the *Estado Novo*, was able to summarize her feelings about 25 April 1974. The new political era heralded by the collapse of the authoritarian regime assiduously created and maintained for over half a century by Dr. Antonio Salazar and his successor Marcello Caetano became immediately significant for the status of women in Portuguese society. Two events can be singled out. First, the case against the "Three Marias"—three Portuguese feminist writers who were arrested and brought to trial in 1972 for publishing a book that was considered an "outrage to public decency,"— was dropped. Although essentially a work of fiction, *As Cartas Novas Portuguesas (New Portuguese Letters)* signaled the rebirth of the Portuguese feminist movement which, although active in the early decades of the twentieth century, was quashed with the advent of the Salazar regime. The letter format of *As Cartas Novas Portuguesas* is based upon the seventeenth-century letters of a Portuguese nun (Sister Mariana Alcoforada) to a French officer with whom she had fallen in love, letters made famous in a 1913 translation by Ranier Maria Rilke. As Helen Lane notes in her preface to the English translation, *The Three Marias*:

> Mariana's convent becomes the symbol of all the walls within which society continues to confine women, a prison today relabeled marriage, motherhood, or a lifelong feminine docility not far removed from the old religious vows of duty, obedience, and self-abnegation. In the imaginary letters composed by the Three Marias, the relations between Mariana and her French cavalier become the symbol of the deep ambivalence underlying the relations between man and woman in all times and places.[14]

Of equal significance for the status of women in the new Portuguese democracy was the formulation of a constitution which proclaimed equality between the sexes at all levels, and the establishment, in Lisbon, of the Commission on the Feminine Condition. The struggle—started by early twentieth-century Portuguese feminists such as Ana Osorio, Adelaide Cabete, and Maria Lamas prior to the creation of the *Estado Novo*—was reopened and new efforts were made to reform many of the laws that had subjugated Portuguese women for over forty years.

During the First Portuguese Republic (1910–1926), certain advances were made to alter the position of women in Portugal, particularly through the Republican League for Portuguese Women, which called for changes such as the initiation of women's suffrage and economic autonomy, and the abolition of antidivorce laws. Adulterers were to be dealt with similarly, whether male or female, and women no longer owed obedience to their husbands within marriage.

The *Estado Novo* reversed many of these new laws to halt the path of progress. The 1933 Constitution established the equality of citizens before the law, except for women who are "different" due to their "nature and for the interest of the family." In 1939, the new Civil Code reestablished a husband's privilege to insist that his wife remain in the home, and in 1946 another law was formulated to deny women the right to vote, granted in 1931. This latter law was not passed, but discrepancies remained until 1968 in the designation of voting eligibility of men as opposed to women. While men were allowed to vote if they simply knew how to read and write, women had to have at least a secondary education. Furthermore, illiterate men were permitted to vote upon payment of an annual tax of at least 100 escudos on capital goods, while women, *if they knew how to read and write*, were required to pay, in addition, a tax of not less than 200 escudos. Needless to say, these laws virtually disenfranchised the major portion of the Portuguese female population.

Until 1969, women in Portugal had no passports of their own and in order to travel abroad they were required to obtain their husband's permission. Furthermore, although this legislation was changed in 1969 to allow a woman to travel freely abroad, it was still illegal for her to travel with her children without the written authorization of her husband. Laws such as these severely restricted the emigration of women, particularly women whose husbands, for whatever reasons, preferred not to have their wives join them in France.

Several other inequalities existed in the Portuguese Civil Code with regard to the legal status of women in Salazarist Portugal: the inability of women to contract debts, to acquire or alienate goods, or to demand separation for male adultery except under special circumstances. Indeed, Portuguese law permitted a man to murder his adulterous wife without prosecution, suggesting simply that he then "disappear" until the incident had blown over. Such liberties were not granted to women! Women were not allowed to act as judges or diplomats or to preside over municipal chambers or village or district councils. These latter laws make the 1979 appointment of the first Portuguese woman Prime Minister even more significant.

While the Civil Code of 1966 gave women the right to exercise freely certain professions and to dispose freely of their salaries, it reestablished the concept of marital power whereby the husband was to be considered as the "head of household" and therefore responsible for all major decisions pertaining to conjugal life. It is the definition of "head of household" that is crucial, since by virtue of this status the male is dominant and represents the family unit to the "outside world." A woman is considered to be the legal head of household only if she is widowed, divorced, legally separated, or single with dependents. Furthermore, in this position she must live "on her own means" and be "morally fit." The only context in which a married woman was able to assume the title of head of household (other than through divorce, legal separation, or widowhood) was when her husband was away or his whereabouts unknown, or when he was unable to act as head of household. The frequent absence of men through emigration in the villages of northern Portugal thus gave Portuguese peasant women a degree of authority and influence denied to women of other classes of Portuguese society. This explains the use of the term "matriarchy" by the Portuguese ethnographer Jorge Dias and the French social historian Descamps in their descriptions of rural life in Portugal. However, peasant wives did not replace their husbands as heads of households, they simple acted as substitutes in their absence.

The subordination of women inherent in Portuguese civil codes was bolstered by the Catholic Church which stood, in the figure of Cardinal Cerejeira, at the right hand of Salazar's *Estado Novo* as a pillar of the reactionary regime. Salazar himself was a religious man who, early in his life, had studied to enter the priesthood and who based his concept of the New State on Catholic principles. The position of the Church under his regime was firmly established with the Concordat of 1940 which, among other things, gave the Church full control over religious education in the schools, recognized only Catholic marriages as legally binding, and repealed the divorce laws promulgated under the First Republic. The Catholic Church reaffirmed its status as the most important national institution at the local level, a status that it had been denied during the anticlerical First Republic.

As in other Catholic countries of western and southern Europe, the Portuguese Church found its major support among the female population and through these women entered into the very soul of the Portuguese family. Religious dogma instilled the values of obedience, submission, and hard work in the hearts of female parishioners. Following the teachings of Saint Paul, the Portuguese Church upheld the authority of the husband in the conjugal unit. A woman's maternal role remained supreme. A book on women published by a Catholic-based organization suggested the following rules of behavior for young wives:

> To be the honest companion of an honest working man, to understand your husband, love him, forgive him his little defects of bad humor, do not demand of him any sacrifices of his dignity, prefer an obscure poverty to an illegitimate wealth, live in the narrow intimacy of your spirit and your heart, forget yourself to live for your spouse and your children . . . this is the divine aspiration which should fill the soul of a true woman.[15]

The sense of abnegation, humility, sacrifice, and acceptance of authority that the Portuguese Catholic Church engendered in at least half of the national population contributed greatly to the strength of the Salazar regime.

One final aspect of this regime that has had important implications for the position of women was its emphasis on social hierarchy and the differences drawn between the poor and illiterate masses and the wealthy, educated members of the upper classes. For women, this difference is clearly outlined in the definition of the Portuguese word *mulher* ("woman") that appears in the *Grande Encyclopaedia Portuguesa e Brasileira*: "uma pessoa de sexo feminino de condição social inferior (por oposição a senhora ou dama)" ("a person of the feminine sex of *inferior social condition* [in opposition to a lady or madame]").[16] To be a *senhora* was held up as an ideal for all Portuguese womanhood, much as the image of the "lady" influenced the aspirations of working-class girls in nineteenth-century England and America.[17] A Portuguese *senhora*'s place was in the home, a factor that led a French traveller in Portugal to make the following observation in the mid 1950s:

> Portuguese women do not occupy the position that they occupy in our country. Portuguese civilization is a male civilization. The women hardly appear, so to speak, in the exterior world.[18]

Portuguese senhoras had maids to do their chores outside the home, and those who were obliged to do the shopping themselves were considered to be "victims of difficult circumstances."[19] The major goal for the Portuguese senhora was to marry and consequently she received little education except in feminine skills. She was expected to "sing, play the piano, wear silk stockings all day in order to satisfy the vanity of [her] husband."[20] Simone de Beauvoir has described these ideals as characteristics of much of Europe during the Victorian era. They have simply survived longer in Portugal, reinforced by Salazarist ideas about social hierarchy.

> Most bourgeois women accepted this gilded confinement and the few who complained were unheard. Bernard Shaw remarks that it is easier to put chains on men than to remove them, if the chains confer benefits. The middle class woman clung to her chains because she clung to the privileges of her class. Freed from the male, she would have to work for a living; she felt no solidarity with working women and she believed that the emancipation of bourgeois women could mean the ruination of her class.[21]

Rural peasant and urban lower-class women who were forced to work out of economic necessity were not confined to the home. But this, in itself, was the stigma of their social position. Legal codes, Church dogma, and certain social values supported under the *Estado Novo* operated together to uphold the ideal domestic role of women and her subordination to the Portuguese male.

CHAPTER TWO

First Story: Ricardina dos Santos

Quando mais tem, mais querem
"The more you have, the more you want"

Not many cultures have a single word that typifies or expresses the fundamental ethos of that culture. The Portuguese, however, can point easily to the word *saudade*, which roughly translates to "nostalgia" or "yearning." *Saudade* is closely connected with emigration, with the yearning that Portuguese emigrants have for their homeland and the hope of returning there one day. When they return, it is to the village where they were born and where they grew to adulthood. They return to the roots of their being; they return to remember.

For Ricardina dos Santos, that village is the hamlet of Seara, deep in the interior province of Beira Alta, a small place as yet untouched by modernization. Seara is wedged in the foothills of the large mountain range, the Serra d'Estrella, which forms the eastern backbone of Portugal. To arrive there, one must leave the road that runs between the provincial towns of Lamego and Trancoso and follow a dirt road that crosses the crests and valleys of the undulating hills. The predominant colors: grey, ochre, and brown, are unsettling to those who are more familiar with the ever-green countryside of the Algarve in southern Portugal or Minho in the northwest. Life here, by contrast, seems harder, the people more isolated, and time more a part of the past than of the present. In this region the peasants cultivate rye, potatoes, and chestnuts. The total absence of vines, which abound in the more coastal areas of

Map of the Village of Seara

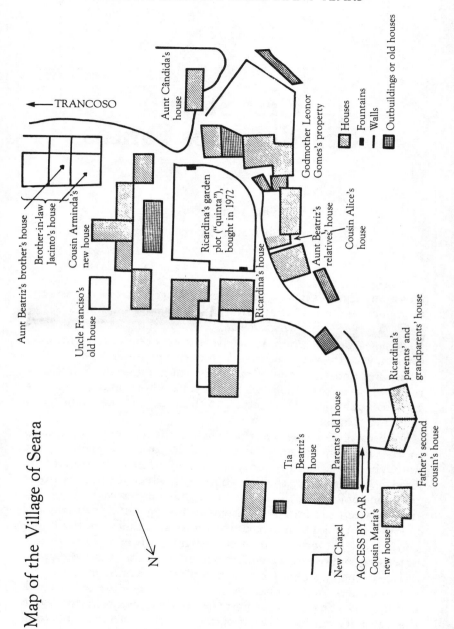

Portugal, suggests a life which is sadder, more onerous, and more dependent upon the temperaments of nature.

Following along the dirt road, one passes through a wood of pine trees. These trees furnish a liquid gold—resin, which the peasants of the region exploit. Then, on a rise in the distant countryside, one catches a glimpse of Seara, a small grouping of houses surrounded by the checkerboard fields of grain and brushwood, peppered here and there with chestnut trees.

Seara is better known by the name Quinta de Seara, "farm of Seara." The title suggests that at some time in the past all the land belonged to a single owner. In 1859, there were five households and twenty-one inhabitants, but today the land is divided among the descendants of these old families and the number of households has expanded to eighteen.[1]

Most of the houses are built of small stones piled together with very little mortar. The only new house in the village is one built by Ricardina's cousin Maria, whose husband, a native of the province of Minho, was the first from Seara to depart for France. Rather than build a new home, Ricardina and her husband have purchased an old house which they use each summer when they return from France for vacation.

Ricardina's mother and father still live in the village, though their four daughters have all departed. Ricardina's eldest sister, Julia, is also in France where she works as a cleaning lady and lives with her husband and two sons. The next oldest, Elsa, is a teacher in Trancoso. The youngest, Rosa, is married to a sailor and lives and works in Lisbon.

Ricardina's husband Manuel was raised in a nearby village. His mother, Ricardina's aunt (Ricardina and Manuel are first cousins as well as spouses), moved to this village when she married Manuel's father. Ricardina and Manuel saw very little of one another while they were growing up because of differences between their respective parents over a plot of land. Manuel is the only son in a family of five children. One of his sisters lives in Africa,[2] working as a seamstress, and her husband works on the railroad. The other three girls are all in France. Two of them are married and the third remains single.

Ricardina and Manuel renewed their acquaintance in France and were married there. Manuel emigrated at the age of sixteen to avoid military service, which, in the early 1960s inevitably would have

Views of Seara, Ricardina's village, September 1975.

entailed service in Africa. His story of clandestine emigration is the story of many young Portuguese men who decided to leave their country during the decade of the 1960s rather than to fight a war which they could not understand and which possibly would have meant giving up as much as four years of their lives. Fortunately, Manuel had a cousin in France who assumed responsibility for him when he first arrived and who provided him with food and shelter until he found work. After that, and until he married, he lived with other young Portuguese on construction sites in Orsay, a bedroom suburb south of the city of Paris where many Portuguese emigrants live and work.

Ricardina emigrated in December 1966 at the age of twenty-one. She met Manuel the following spring and in April 1968 they were married. Today, Ricardina and Manuel live in a concierge apartment in the seventeenth arrondissement of Paris. It is more spacious than most concierge apartments. The living room is dominated by a large television set and one corner is curtained off to hide the bed that Ricardina and Manuel share. Their two sons, both born in France, sleep in a second room above the living room. These two rooms are adjoined by a small circular stair. The dining room is formally furnished with a table and two buffets. On the walls are family photographs and various knicknacks. A small kitchen and private bath (a luxury where Portuguese concierges are concerned) complete the apartment.

Ricardina's migration represents one pattern of Portuguese female migration: that of young single women who emigrate to earn money to help their parents, their siblings, or themselves; or who leave in order to escape a village way of life which is more onerous and socially restrictive for young women than for young men. It is a migration partly precedented in the internal movement of Portuguese peasant girls to work as domestic servants for wealthy urban families in Porto, Lisbon, or the local provincial town.

Ricardina's entire story is rich in details of Portuguese peasant life and of the life of a peasant girl, several of which deserve some comment before her tale begins. Perhaps the most salient feature is the distaste that she expresses for the *críticas do povo*, the wagging tongues of local gossips which act as a forceful mechanism of social control. This gossip was one of the major reasons for her own emigration, along with a certain shame she felt at being abandoned by a suitor. In her own way, Ricardina forcefully reiterates comments

The Parisian apartment building where Ricardina lives and works as a concierge.

Ricardina dos Santos, June 1980.

made a century ago by the social realist novelist Julio Dinis through his character Daniel in *As Pupillas do Senhor Reitor:*

> This life of the village. This life of slander and of gossip. The misfortune of small places where there are few serious things to think about. Look what these people occupy themselves with: in knowing what I do, how I live, where I go, with whom I speak; this is what entertains them.[3]

Such gossip, in Ricardina's view, and in the view of several ethnographers who have addressed the problem in peasant societies elsewhere in the world, is designed to uphold moral codes as well as to keep everyone in their place. On the one hand, Ricardina is criticized for buying a watch and cutting her hair, both of which represents to fellow villagers her desire to be better than they are, to be a senhora when she is not a senhora. All of the choices that Ricardina makes to take her away from village life, including her final emigration to France, are attempts to improve herself and can be compared to the desires of many other Portuguese women who view migration as an opportunity to move out of the status of a *mulher do campo* ("peasant woman") and into that of a senhora ("lady"), or at least a *dona da casa* ("housewife"). As noted in the previous chapter, this change in status is extremely important in a country like Portugal where social hierarchy has remained rigidly defined throughout the Salazar regime and where titles and forms of address (including the titles of senhora and dona) are a major means to distinguish those who work with their hands from those who do not. "In my country," the journalist Antonio de Figueiredo has written, "to be poor is like being a member of a caste."[5]

On the other hand, Ricardina is the brunt of gossip for some of her activities within the intricate ritual of Portuguese courtship, a subject about which she elaborates in great detail.[6] In Portugal, courting practices are perhaps less formalized, particularly in comparison with Spain, but there is a definite point when a boy and a girl make their relation public by becoming *namorados* ("lovers" in a neutral sense) or *conversados* (from *conversar*—"to converse"). The period of *namoro* is one of the most important times in a Portuguese girl's life because it is the first step towards the altar and the change in role that marriage signifies.

Namorados send letters to one another during the week and on Sundays the boy comes to visit. They spend the afternoons talking to one another on the doorstep of the girl's house. Whereas in Spain there is often a stigma attached to breaking off this "conversing" relationship, a young girl in Portugal may have several *namorados* during her adolescent years. Thus the following popular rhyme:

> *Amor se te fores embora*
> *Não fica a praia deserta*
> *Vai um amor; fica outra*
> *Não hà palavra mais certo*[7]

> "Lover if you were to leave me
> The beach would not be deserted
> If one love goes another remains
> There is nothing more certain"

However, for the duration of each *namoro* a girl remains faithful to a particular young man. Only when a young girl is *prometida* ("promised") and the young man is allowed into her home does the relationship become truly serious.

This ability to change *namorados* several times throughout adolescence is what necessitates the kind of social control that gossip provides to uphold the values of virginity and chastity, which are as important—at least rhetorically—in Portugal as they are in the rest of Mediterranean Europe and Latin America.

> *Rosa que estas na roseira*
> *Deixa-te estar em botão*
> *Que a rosa depois de aberta*
> *Perde toda a estimação*[8]

> "O Rose on the rosebush
> Remain as a bud
> For a rose after opening
> Loses all esteem"

In addition to gossip, the concept of shame, *vergonha*, is equally powerful in controlling the behavior of women. Shame operates as much in what one writer has referred to as the "ethnically neutral sense" (as modesty, shyness, embarrassment in public) as it does with reference to sexuality.

In its association with sexuality, a girl and her family are shamed if she loses her virginity prior to marriage. A married woman who commits adultery is shameful whereas this is much less serious for men. A woman who is approached by another man should tell her husband about it because if she does not he will become suspicious. According to one Portuguese male, it is up to the Portuguese woman to control her sexual instincts (through shame) because the man is the weaker sex.

> A man is more easily tempted and temptation is a woman's fault. Women have to be strong, to keep their life in order by guarding their virginity and their purity. You can offer a piece of meat to a dog and he takes it. You think that is fine, he is normal. But if he does not want it, you think he is sick. It is the same with women. If some woman suggests that I go off with her, then it is only normal for me to go. I am weak. It is a force of wills, not physical strength that is important. Women must have a strong will to say no because men do not.

Ricardina mentions feelings of shame at many points in her narrative, but the power that both gossip and specific codes of morality have over her life is perhaps made most poignantly in her description of proving her virginity to her husband. Indeed, it was only after I confronted Ricardina as tactfully as possible about the time discrepancy between her marriage and the birth of her first child that she told me this story. One has to wonder whether this "error of memory" was a deliberate omission made so as not to contradict the self that she had chosen to present—a self subjected to *unjustified* gossip.

Although Ricardina's past almost returns to haunt her, of the three women, she is perhaps the most ambitious and the most aware of the differences between her own life and that of her mother. Marriages are no longer arranged, land is no longer valued as the only source of economic security, prosperity, and social prestige, and the traditional rural Portuguese family is slowly eroding as increasing numbers of young people, male and female, have chosen to emigrate in search of a better future.

Despite the geographical and social distance that separates Ricardina from her mother, she still retains strong emotional attachments. She remembers most the sacrifices that her mother made and the work that went into raising a family in conditions of relative hardship. Her preoccupation with illness—her parents' and her own—is symptomatic of a general concern among peasant people with conditions of health. If good health is lacking, all is lacking. Thus, once emigrants in France have saved up money to build a house, they think of working a little longer to put money aside in the event of illness.

All three women whose stories are presented here received only minimal education and were jettisoned early into helping their families economically. Ricardina's description of the conflicts between schooling and work are representative of the general lack of education among the remote populations of rural Portugal until quite recently. Only in 1960 was a minimum of four years of schooling for all Portuguese children made obligatory by the state. Education beyond the primary level remained costly for many rural families because it often involved transportation, room, and board. Antonio Figueiredo has referred to the Portuguese system of education under the *Estado Novo* as feudal, as "an instrument of privilege and discrimination" while Herminio Martins has argued quite bluntly that the lack of educational opportunities for the lower classes of Portuguese society during the Salazar regime was a major result of the cultural immobility of the nation as a whole and an important stimulus for emigration.

If schooling was generally lacking for the lower classes, the situation was even more serious for women. Even among the upper classes, the only kind of education available until quite recently was an education that generally trained them in "feminine skills." According to the 1970 national census, 38.7 percent of Portuguese women over twenty were illiterate, 19.2 percent had at least some primary education and 27.6 percent had completed primary education. Only 7.9 percent had completed any more than primary school. This can be compared with figures for Portuguese men over twenty: 25.1 illiterate, 14.5 percent with some primary schooling, 40.1 percent with a completed primary education, and 13.2 percent with more than a primary education. In 1970, 58 percent of women over fifty were illiterate compared with 40.4 percent of the men.

Among rural parents in particular there was little interest in sending daughters to learn how to read or write because they thought that this would only encourage them to write love letters. What else was writing for? If a girl was lucky enough to go to school, whenever there was work to be done at home she remained at home. Furthermore, once it became necessary to exercise greater supervision over a girl, it was more practical to keep her at home if schooling was unavailable in the village itself. To some extent, as indicated in Ricardina's story, educational opportunities depended on birth order. Thus an eldest daughter very rarely had any schooling since she soon became surrogate mother to her younger siblings.

Prior to her emigration to France, Ricardina spent several years in domestic service in Portugal. A class of rural servant girls became quite common throughout western Europe in the eighteenth and nineteenth centuries, a factor that led Ravenstein, an early migration theorist, to conclude that women are, in fact, more migratory than men over short distances. In Portugal, as elsewhere in western Europe, it was not unusual for a girl to leave her paternal home to seek employment outside the family unit, whether in the home of a wealthier farming family in the same or a nearby village, or in the home of a bourgeois or aristocratic family in a nearby town, or even in the capital city. Until quite recently, as one author has noted, the "entire way of life of the middle and upper classes of Portugal was based upon the existence of an army of women, young and old, who had no other possibilities for work and who therefore formed an inexhaustible supply of cheap labor."[9] In 1950, 71.5 percent of women employed in the tertiary sector of Portugal were employed in *serviços pessoais e domésticas*; 61.1 percent in 1960; 60 percent in 1970.

Although the pay was very low, a period of several years as a servant did enable a young girl from the countryside to provide for herself in the form of a trousseau, accumulating enough to make herself eligible for marriage. However, a village girl who went to serve in the provincial town or in the city also took her reputation into her own hands, and with that the chances of making a good marriage. Young village men often doubted the virginity of serving girls who had spent so much time away from parental supervision. And even if virginity was not the issue, they often thought that a girl who had spent time in the city developed pretensions of being better than they, of being more worldly.

Ricardina contemplated emigration for some time as her last chance to escape village life, but her final decision to leave was made quite suddenly as a result of personal differences with a suitor. Her description of the "illusion" that has brought many people to France is both insightful and philosophical, and, in essence, summarizes the dream of El Dorado that has enticed her compatriots for more than a century. This dream is not simply one of sheer lucre, she tells us, but of lucre in relative terms—relative to oneself, but more importantly, to others. As Figueiredo has written, "For [the Portuguese] people, the possibility of emigration. . . , and perhaps returning one day rich enough to buy the best house and the best land in the neighborhood, and to make friends with the local priest, and other wealthy returned [emigrants] was the only achievement that was really worth hoping for."[10] Ricardina herself mentions the emigrants who return to boast of this or that apocryphal success. The desire for social mobility—or at least the emphasis upon the symbols of social prestige and success—are fundamental to the migration ideology and, it could be argued, a direct result of the fossilized social system within Portugal that has denied social mobility to the essentially peasant migrant population.[11]

Although Ricardina's own migration may have been motivated initially by a desire for freedom and independence, she is clearly swept up by the possibility for social advancement. The frequent mobility that she experiences in France—in places of residence and in jobs—is a result of the desire to get ahead, to look for a better position and better pay. Her ambition to buy real estate in a provincial town in Portugal is one expressed by many Portuguese women, single and married, and one clearly recognized by realtors in Portugal who address advertisements in Portuguese newspapers specifically to *os emigrantes*.

The expectation of returning to Portugal that this ambition involves is, as mentioned earlier, common among Portuguese immigrants in France regardless of whether it will ever become reality. It is common because it involves nostalgia as well as ambition. Ricardina's feelings are indeed feelings of *saudade*: of leaving, adapting, striving for what others have, but never disdaining what is one's own. Thus we return to the village of Seara where Ricardina begins.

I do not have many memories of my mother's father. He died when I was quite small. But I do remember my mother's mother very well. When I was young, I used to spend the night with her. She was all alone and liked my company. Every night, after supper, she would teach me how to pray. She also taught me how to spin with a distaff and spindle so that I could make the thread that she later wove into linen. I remember the deaths of all my grandparents, but most of all hers. We had to summon all the sons and daughters from the villages in the area. She lay for twenty four hours before she was buried and I remember crying a lot. Then they took the coffin on their shoulders and carried it to the next village to be buried. We walked two kilometers to the cemetery.

My father's family has always lived in Seara itself but my mother, before she was married, lived outside the village on a farm that my grandparents rented. My father courted her there. He went at night, but my grandparents never allowed them to be alone together. My mother told me that sometimes, when she had to go to Seara on an errand, my father would follow her, trying to talk alone with her. But she always hurried so that he would not catch up because she was afraid of what people would say if they saw them alone together. They hardly knew one another; on the wedding night, when my mother was preparing for bed she was very nervous because she had never been alone with my father before.

In the past it was the parents who always arranged the marriages. My father, at that time, wanted to be a policeman, but his parents did not allow it. They were afraid that if he left he would never return or that something might happen to him. Instead they encouraged him to marry my mother. They were married in the clothes they used to wear on Sundays. What poverty!

After they were married, my parents moved into Seara. We lived in three different houses while I was growing up. The first was very small with two rooms and an entrance hall. My sisters and I slept in one room, two to a bed, and my parents slept in the other. We never imagined that there were houses where each person has his own room and his own bed. I remember the last house best. There were three rooms and a parlor (*sala*). We paid rent to the owner who lived in Trancoso. It was a bigger house, but even so, there were no windows and no chimney. The smoke in the kitchen escaped through the gaps in the roof. My mother never had nice furniture; she had only what was indispensable and most of that was ugly. A village house is no place for nice things. My father, if he had some extra money, always thought of buying another small plot of land, never, as we do now, of building a nicer house. Today we think differently; we know about things that they never imagined existed when they were young.

When I was a little girl, we had two small plots of our own and then several others that we rented. My father was amazing and always very astute in governing his life. He began with very little, but in the end he cultivated more fields and harvested more potatoes than anyone else, even more than my godmother who was the richest person in the village. People always talked about my father—they said that he was lucky. They never recognized that it was with hard work that he improved himself. Today the land my father and mother work is all their own. They have inherited from their parents. But today, because of emigration, there are not enough people to help them with the work and some of the land remains uncultivated.

My parents would be rich if they had not had so many problems and disasters in their lives. They were both ill and lost a fortune with their ailments. You might say that it was my father who caused my mother's illness. She was pregnant with my youngest sister and unwell. She did her housework, but only a little and she often had to lie down to rest. My father went out alone to work in the fields. One day, he returned with the donkey laden with potatoes. He arrived at the door of the house and did not see my mother because she was resting. He became very nervous and excited and began to untie the sacks of potatoes hurriedly. My mother saw that he was angry at having to do the work alone and went out to help him. She put her hands under one of the big sacks so that it would not fall to the ground. My father, because he was working so quickly, let the sack fall suddenly into her hands. It gave a blow to her stomach and she became very ill. We had only a little money saved and had to spend all of it on medicine.

Soon after, my father also became ill. One Saturday he was packing the underbrush onto the ox cart and he fell off. From that point on, he suffered with a stomach ailment and could no longer work hard. We had to hire servants to work alongside my sisters and I in the fields.[12]

Our life as children was one of always helping my parents. My sister Julia, the eldest, was the farmer, not my father. She was the workhorse. Perhaps it was for this reason that she married so young—at seventeen—to flee my parents' house and all the work that they gave her. She was never allowed to do anything. She liked to go to dances, but my father always insisted that the work be finished. She cried all the time and probably thought that in her own house she would be freer.

Julia was a pretty girl, with flowing hair. She had many suitors including a cousin of ours who wanted to marry her and take her to Brazil. No one in the family wanted her to go and so she stayed. Her husband—my brother-in-law—is also from Seara. Before they married, my brother-in-law completed his military service. My sister wore a ring he had given her before leaving for the army, and they wrote to each other while he was away. My mother and god-mother were not in favor of the marriage because they said that my brother-in-law drank too much wine. But Julia insisted and finally everyone agreed. The day of the wedding came, but they could not get married because my brother-in-law had not secured all the proper papers.[13] It was shameful! However, my mother had already prepared the wedding feast and eighty people had come to the house. That night my brother-in-law wanted to sleep with my sister. My mother at first refused because they were not married. She said to my brother-in-law, "Today I will give you my daughter and to-morrow you will leave her." My brother-in-law replied, "If I do not sleep with her today, I will go away and never return!" Everyone had to agree and they spent the next eight days together before they could be married in Church. My mother suffered a great deal at that time but soon the grandchildren began to come and it was a great joy for all of us. Later, when my mother began to feel more and more ill, she came to fear that she would not see the rest of us married and settled in our own lives.

Today I think about my mother a great deal. I think of her, poor thing, full of work and alone. A mother is the most important person in one's life. One never forgets the sacrifices she makes. It is as in a song we used to sing:

> Ó minha mãe, minha amada
> Quem tem uma, tem tudo
> Ó minha mãe, minha amada
> Quem a não tem, não tem nada

"O my mother, O my love
Whoever has a mother has everything
O my mother, O my love
Whoever has no mother has nothing."

I feel sorry for my father too, but it is not the same feeling. My father always scolded us; he was more severe and we were afraid of him. He had "that character" that all men of the country have. I remember one time when my sister Rosa and I went with my mother to my grandmother's house. Lunch time arrived and my mother told us to return to the house to start the meal before my father returned from the fields. I told my sister "you go!" She told me "you go!" The time passed, my mother finished the work she had to do, and the three of us went home together. We hurried to prepare the meal, but that day my father arrived back earlier than we had expected. "So, it is only now that you are preparing the meal," he said. My mother told him that she had instructed us to return home earlier but that we had not obeyed her. My father became very angry. "Three women in the house and the meal is not ready!" he shouted. He took off his belt and hit me above the lips and my sister on the back. The blood began to flow. I was ashamed to go out after that because people would ask me who had hit me. When we were younger my father never beat us with his belt, but that time, as we were more grown up, he did. A father has all the authority and if it is necessary to shout or to beat, he will.

I have respect for this kind of education and will give it to my own children. I want them to obey me, and if they do not I will spank them. Boy or girl, I am always demanding—as my parents were with me.

Meu pai é cantadeiro
Minha mãe é cantadeira
Eu sou filha deles ambos
Eu sigo a mesma carreira.

"My father is a singer
My mother is a songstress
I am the child of them both
I will follow the same career"

In the village almost everyone is family and when some poor beggar or fool appeared from outside we always laughed at him. I remember a crazy woman who was called "Stupid Ana"; at least, that was the name we gave her when we were children. She used to go about begging and we would yell after her to frighten her. She always carried a big stick with which to defend herself. Another old beggar used to sleep in the bread oven and ate whatever he could get his hands on. But instead of accepting any charity, he would exchange things. The tinsmith also used to come from time to time to repair pots and pans, and the basketmaker to repair old baskets. Nowadays, these people no longer exist because everyone has enough money to buy new things. As children, however, they were our only contact with the outside world. It was not until I went to school that I really began to learn my way about, to see new places, new people, and new things.

My sister Elsa took me to school the first day. She already knew everyone and went wherever she pleased. I followed her about and was embarrassed until I knew more people. We walked to school and it took about an hour to get there. Sometimes there were great storms and we became very wet. Our teacher was never kind and had little patience with us. One time we asked for her permission to attend communion services on the following day but she did not give it. Several of us missed school that day and the next day we tried to make it up to her by bringing fruit and cheese to school. She beat us and some parents talked about making a complaint. They never did. In Portugal there are few good teachers who care about children in the villages. Perhaps for this reason I never continued on. I was very lazy and had to repeat the first year because I failed arithmetic. My father knew how to read a little but he never helped me and my mother still cannot read. When we arrived home we never had time for our homework as children do today. There was always farm work to be done. I never had a good head for studies and it was not worthwhile for my parents to pay for my education. After the third year I dropped out, since even a fourth year was not obligatory then.

At the time I began school, we also began to carry the mail for Seara and the surrounding villages. We earned something by taking charge of this task, but not much. My father asked for a mail delivery to Seara because there was none and it was necessary to travel the three miles to Trancoso to pick it up. When we took over the mail delivery, it was often my responsibility to take the sack from village to village. I did it on my way to and from school. I was only seven when I had this duty to perform.

I never had a head for studying but I always wanted to learn something so that I would not have to remain all my life in the countryside. My sister Elsa had her chance. There was a teacher who encouraged her to study to become a teacher herself. My mother agreed because she liked to see my sister learning. Since my mother could not handle all the housework alone I remained at home to help her. Once I asked my mother to let me study embroidery and she agreed because she thought that I should learn some skill too. But if there was a lot of work to be done on any day, I did not go to the classes. I never finished the course and have had little practice. I wanted to pursue something to the end, no matter what, and then teach it someday, but I never had the chance. I was imprisoned by my parents and worked like an ox.

Nevertheless, I still began to think about my trousseau and when I had time in the evenings I embroidered the sheets and tablecloths that were necessary. A girl in Portugal has to think about these things. Otherwise she will marry and have nothing. I began also to think about earning a bit of extra money for myself and, when the chance arose to go to serve for a family outside the village, I begged my parents to let me go.

My cousin Antonio was taking care of the farm of some rich people and found me a position in their house as a maid. They wanted a person whom they could trust. I was seventeen when I left Seara for Castelo Rodrigo, a provincial town about fifty miles away. My employer was a lawyer. I was the first servant they hired but, soon after, they employed another girl to work in the kitchen and I just waited on tables, made the beds, and did the shopping. The other maid and I shared a room on the ground floor. We slept there side by side. Soon I began to feel homesick. There were always little differences that upset me. Once, for example, I was making the bed for the lady of the house and speaking of her little boy, I called him "Zeco" instead of "zequinho."[14] She scolded me because I had not used the appropriate name. One day, I decided to leave. I told my employers I was getting married and returned as soon as possible to my parents.

It was while I was serving in Castelo Rodrigo that I cut my hair. It was a very significant thing because no woman has short hair in the village. I told my parents that my employer had insisted that I cut my hair, but when I arrived in Seara I was criticized. People of the countryside think that women with short hair are not serious, that they are loose. But this was not the first time that I had been criticized. I was also the first in the village to buy a watch. People thought that the money I had spent on the watch could have been better used. A watch, like fine handkerchiefs, scarves for one's hair, silk stockings, pants or face powder were considered to be things only for fine ladies (senhoras). And we were not fine ladies. Everything was censured. People in the village were always jealous of our family and gossipped about us. Perhaps they said bad things about me for even going to serve as a maid, but as more and more girls followed in my footsteps, it became less "evil."

Later, my cousin returned to say that he knew a senhora in Trancoso who needed someone to help her with a baby. I went to Trancoso to serve again, and later I accompanied the child and the young couple to Porto where the senhora's mother-in-law lived. Life in Porto with this family was very different from anything I had known before. People lived in cleaner surroundings and in cleaner clothes. I began to earn money and to learn about life in the city.

Then the senhora's husband went to London and she went with him. I stayed with the baby and the senhora's mother, who had one house in Trancoso and another in Lisbon. We went to Lisbon and remained there until the senhora came from London to take her child with her. In Lisbon, there were two other maids; one for the kitchen and the other to do the cleaning. My sole responsibility was the child, although sometimes I helped the others. Soon, as in the house in Castelo Rodrigo, there arose a point of contention. One day I was combing the little girl's hair and I noticed that it was very long in the front. Her hair was falling over her eyes and I thought it looked ugly. I cut a bit off. When the child's grandmother came in and saw the hair shorter she began to shout, "Who cut the child's hair?" All of us were afraid to speak but I finally admitted to it. She scolded me sharply and I cried.

The next day we had to go to Porto to visit with the other grandmother. I was scolded during the entire trip and when we arrived, my employer went quickly into the house with the child. I came behind with all the luggage. When I arrived the two women had already discussed the matter. The Porto woman said that there was no reason to be so upset about such a trifle. I was pleased with her because she understood that it was nothing and I would never do anything to hurt the child. But it is during times like this that you realize you are best off in your own house with your own family. You learn that it requires a great deal of patience to serve others. Everytime I wrote home, I cried and one day I decided to return there for good. I never served again in Portugal.

I am going to tell a story about a cousin, the daughter of my mother's sister in Conceicao. Her name is Odette and she is about my age. When she was younger, her parents kept her in a kind of captivity. They never let her go to dances even though she loved to dance. They never let her do anything. But the harder the parents are, the worse are the things that their children do. Odette went to work for my godmother and there she fell in love with one of the young men who used to tend my godmother's sheep. One day he asked her to marry him and she accepted because she wanted to leave her parents' house for good. The young man knew that he would be better off by marrying her because he was much poorer than she was. One day, they were together and they "did the thing" and she became pregnant. Certainly she must have done it because her parents were against the marriage. One day at mass she told her mother that she was pregnant. Her mother told her father and he fell into a fury. He went to my godmother's house straight away in search of the young man. Odette hid under the bed when she heard her father coming. The young man had gone out into the fields with my godfather to spray the potatoes. My godfather knew nothing of what had happened, but he saw my uncle coming and told the young man to flee. He fled into the mountains.

While my uncle was chasing the young man, my aunt was searching for Odette throughout the village. Odette went home, packed some of her things, including her jewelry, and fled to join her lover. She found him in the house of friends in Trancoso. Everyone talked about this event a great deal. A girl who does a thing like this is an embarrassment to everyone. But soon, Odette married the young man and people began to talk less about it. Only after four or five years did my aunt begin to visit her daughter in Trancoso, without my uncle's knowledge. Today, however, both of them are older and they need their daughter so everyone is friendly again. Odette's husband knows how to govern his life well and they have been fairly successful. In the end, it was better that they married. It would have been worse for Odette if the young man had left her with the baby in her arms.

For me it was different. I never did anything like Odette did but I was criticized nevertheless and found myself having to evade the tongues of neighbors. In these small places, people are brutish. Everyone knows about everyone else and there are many obstacles in love. The life of a girl in such places is a constant struggle against criticism and gossip. To gossip about a boy, he must be a drunkard, or someone who plays cards or smokes heavily. But the smallest thing in a girl's behavior is criticized. A girl who wants to dress herself in a modern style is criticized. A boy who does not like her that way begins to talk. He is afraid that she will become too much of a lady for him. When my sister Elsa began to study to become a teacher, people said that she was mixing with people who were not her kind. They were jealous. I do not know why people always talked about my sisters and I most of all. Perhaps it was because we had no brother to protect us. Other boys who are afraid of a girl's brother will not talk about her.

I remember once when I cried a lot because of the vicious gossip. I always had many suitors and the other girls were jealous. They used to invent stories so that the suitors would leave me. At one time, I used to see a fellow who came from a nearby village. His name was Alcides. There were others at that time who were interested in me, but I was only interested in this one boy. One fine Sunday, a distant cousin of mine came through Seara. He was married and lived in Trancoso. I had never met him before but had heard people talking about him saying that he was a man who liked women.

My sister Julia had a small tavern in the village and that Sunday this cousin went into the tavern to have something to drink. At that time I was working in my godmother's house and I went to get some water from the well. On the way back I stopped into the tavern as was my habit. My sister was downstairs in the kitchen. This cousin and the other young men were there together drinking. Soon my cousin rose to leave. As my sister was downstairs, she did not see him leaving so I approached him to take the money for the drink. I used to help my sister in this way. The other men there, because they were jealous of my boyfriend Alcides, invented a story about this cousin giving me 500 escudos to tempt me down the road of sin. They invented the story so Alcides would leave me.

During the following week, I heard from all sides "and the 500 and the 500". I did not understand what they were talking about until the following Sunday when Alcides arrived to visit me. He asked me to give him back his letters, the ones he had written to me. I asked him why and he responded that I should know very well why. I told him that I had no idea why he was angry so he told me about the gossip he had heard. I took him to my sister's so that she could put the story right, telling him that if he did not believe her then I did not care and he could have his letters back. My sister thought that we should make a complaint to the tribunal because such gossip could have been the ruin of me. They talked about it everywhere.

This all happened in the summer and Alcides stopped seeing and talking to me. In February he went into the army, but just before leaving he began to visit me once more. I told him that I could not be *namorados* with him anymore because my parents were opposed to it. A cousin of mine knew him well and said that he played cards and drank a bit. My parents were worried that I would not be happy with him. My father even threatened to beat me if he saw me with Alcides again. I obeyed him because I did not want to cause a scandal.

I had other suitors after Alcides, but was not interested in any of them until I met Jorge. But it was Jorge who made me decide to emigrate for France. He had been my boyfriend for quite awhile before his time for military service came up. I waited for him on the Saturday before he was due to leave for Lisbon and Angola but he did not come by. The next day I went to help my sister Elsa the teacher. She lived in the same village as Jorge. There was a dance and I went to find him there and speak with him. But he would not dance with me, nor speak to me. He told me that he had heard certain things about me but he would not tell me exactly what. That week, after he had left, I wrote a letter which must have reached him in Lisbon before he embarked for Africa. The letter even made my mother cry. I told him that whatever he had heard about me was a lie. I opened my heart to him and he forgave me and wrote from Africa.

He returned from Africa at the time when there was a party for the people in the embroidery class. I invited him to the festa. But instead of dancing with me he danced with another girl. I did not try to talk to him because I was afraid of what other people would say. I became so nervous and angry that I went that afternoon to arrange with someone to take me to France. My sister Julia was already abroad, and I had been thinking about the idea for quite some time, but Jorge was the one who made up my mind for me. I never had a chance to talk to him before leaving and my sister Elsa advised me not to write from France. I left Portugal in December of 1966 and in August of the following year I heard that Elsa had married Jorge. She told me later what had happened.

Jorge's mother did not know that I had been seeing her son. One day she went to talk to my sister Elsa and suggested that Elsa marry her son. My sister wrote to me about it and I said that I was no longer interested in him. They began to see each other and liked one another. But later on, as all the papers for marriage were being finalized, Elsa began to have her doubts about him. When she wrote again it was already too late. My sister Julia, who was in France too, returned in August to help with the wedding. She was very excited about it. Things happened too quickly and Elsa was too ashamed by that time to send Jorge on his way. She was afraid of what people would say about it. If she had written to me earlier I would have told her not to marry him if she was hesitant. She could have joined me in France, fled as I fled. But it was all too late.

After they were married, nothing went well. He was never a tender man. Today they live a little better but argue occasionally. He only knows how to work in a store, that is all. Perhaps it would have been better if I had married him instead of her. I might have made a different person of him. But in the end, my destiny was different; France changed my life.

Emigrants leave for this reason: the life of the fields is nothing. They work a lot and they have nothing. They sell a bushel of potatoes or beans for nothing. Everything they grow is worth little. For those people with many children and little land, France was a salvation. But France is also an illusion that made many people leave a good life there in Portugal; a big illusion to come and earn money, nothing more. Many thought that they would come to France for a short time, make their fortune and leave. The first few years are difficult, but then they begin to like it and do not want to go back so soon. They reach a point where they have money to build a new house but then they decide to stay a few more years in order to buy a car or a small business. Time passes. They count on being abroad three or four years and instead stay six or eight. The more they have, the more they want. The more they see in the bank, the more they want to put there. They never stop working, they never leave France.

There are Portuguese men and women in France who return over the vacation to Portugal and make themselves out to be more than they are. They lie, saying they are master of this or that in France, when the truth is that they clean offices and washrooms. Sometimes they do work that is worse than what their counterparts do in Portugal. I have met people in the consulate who are trying to fix their passports so that they can go home. Some say they regret leaving the life they had in Portugal. When they arrive they cannot speak the language, they cannot find a job or housing, they cannot secure the proper papers. They waste their lives. France has been good for some, but it is the ruination of others.

I came to France with the same illusions but they were complicated by the problems with my suitors. I also wanted to be free, to break out of my parents' house for good. I was always bored with the life in the countryside and was looking for a more respectable way of life. It did not matter to me if I went to serve in a house because I saw that I could not improve my life through studies. When I returned from Lisbon, I worked like a slave for my parents but earned nothing and could enjoy nothing. France was my chance to change all this.

My brother-in-law Jacinto went to France first and then later my sister Julia joined him. I began to write letters to her to see if she could arrange work for me. In one letter she would tell me that she had found something, but in the next she would write that it was impossible. I became very discouraged and began to think that I would never be able to leave. Then when Jorge and I broke up I decided to leave anyway. I went to talk to one of my ex-boyfriends who was working as a chauffeur. He told me that he was afraid to take me himself because the police were imprisoning people who were acting as guides (passadores), but he found another man who was willing to take me. At first my parents were against the idea because they thought something might happen to me, especially if I went all alone with this strange man. But I assured them that another woman would accompany us and that no harm would come to me. Finally they agreed.

The man who was going to guide me asked for a photograph and some money, which my father borrowed for me. In six months I had paid back what I owed for the voyage. One night the man came to get me and took me in a car to Vila Formosa near the Spanish border. Before we had entered the town he told me to get out of the car and to follow another man on foot. I followed him at a distance because I was frightened and did not trust him completely. But the next thing I knew, I was in Spain. I got into the car again with the man and the other woman and everything went well as we drove through Spain. Then we had to get out of the car again. We ran into some police and I became quite frightened because I had no passport. But they were kind and helped us. We were already in France.

It was 10 December 1966. I only had the address of my brother-in-law's factory. But it was a Sunday and the factory was closed. The woman who had traveled with me said that I could stay with her that night. The next morning I found my brother-in-law and later we went home to my sister. I stayed with them for eight days until I found work in the house of a neighbor of my sister's employer. I worked two hours a day but I had to find more work in order to secure working papers. Soon I had a job replacing a Spanish woman who had returned to Spain for the holidays. She never returned to France so I took over the post permanently. I worked two hours in the morning and four during the afternoon; six hours at five francs (approx $1.00) an hour. By then I was sleeping in the house of my sister's employer, in a sixth-floor room. Later I changed rooms and paid for my new place with an hour of work a day. I moved a third time a few months later into a room owned by the woman for whom I worked in the afternoons. I worked two hours for the room and two hours for myself.

In the beginning I was very enthusiastic about France. I felt very free. Even today I sometimes cry about the time I have left behind, the time when I was single, earned my own money, and could do what I wanted to do. But one must understand this kind of freedom because in coming to France we also leave a certain freedom behind, the freedom of the countryside where everyone works for themselves. Everything they have is their own. They can rest when they want to, work when they want to. People arrive in France and enclose themselves in small rooms with only electric light. They pass through the entire year without seeing the sun, worrying each day about getting to work on time.

Many things about France impressed me at first, but above all it was the French who "made love" in the streets, on the metro, on buses, anywhere. It made me ashamed because I had never seen it in

Portugal where people are more discreet. There were other little things that were different. In Portugal we never carry a loaf of bread in our hand. It is always wrapped up or in a sack. I never painted my nails or my lips in Portugal. A friend whom I met here insisted to me that it was not a bad thing, but because I was not used to it I had a hard time accustoming myself to it. When I went out with lipstick on, it seemed to me as if everyone was staring at me.

When I left Portugal for France, I had a particular idea in mind: to earn money and to be independent. Life in France was liberating at first but then it began to change. I came to France with no intention of finding a boyfriend or a husband. I wanted to make my life on my own but soon there were new suitors and I was no longer in peace. The first young man was a friend of my brother-in-law's. I was afraid to go out with him because he had no papers and could not return to Portugal. Besides, he was too young and "stylish" for me. Later, there was a young man who was very persistent in his pursuit of me. One day, I went to the market and he followed me, although I did not realize it at the time. When I returned to my room, he asked my niece and nephews who were playing outside who I was. I came out again and he wished me good day, calling me by name. I went on walking without responding to him but he continued to speak to me. "Well, you do not know me," he said. "I am from Castelo (a village near Seara), son of so-and-so. I was three when I left for Lisbon but I know you because I used to hunt in the country and saw you there." I knew the family he had mentioned but did not know him. He followed me to my sister's house while my niece and nephews ran before me shouting that I already had a boyfriend! This young man began to speak to my sister about becoming engaged to me. He had no shame! I told him no, that I had not thought of marrying and that I had no trousseau. He said that did not matter and continued to pursue me. One day I became very angry. I called him an "authentic man of the streets" and sent him on his way. After him there were others, but no one who interested me until I met Manuel. He is my first cousin but until then I hardly knew him. One day I went with my sister to Orsay where he was living with some friends. He liked me that day and later came to visit me but no one would have said that we were courting because I did not speak to him in particular.

Then on Easter Sunday my sister and I organized a party and many people in the family came. My sister's employer had left on vacation and we prepared a big meal and people slept there in the house. The next morning we went into the city and my cousin stayed close to me and began to talk of love. If I had told him no, he would never have come back; so I did not say no. I already knew him and trusted him more than the other men. I knew that he was a good person whom I could respect. Only afterwards did the problems arise.

My mother-in-law was against the marriage, not only because we were first cousins, but also because she and my parents had had a difference over a plot of land back in Portugal. I knew she was against it because she would not send the proper papers and my husband finally had to return to Portugal himself to arrange everything. When he went back, he heard a lot of bad things about me. He told me that the more bad things he heard, the more he liked me; but there was always some doubt nourished by the things that people in the village were filling his ears with. It was necessary to give him certainty before he would marry me and I did "it" with many tears. Even today I regret what I did but there is no remedy for it. I was married in April of 1968 and my first son was born in October of the same year. I married in France because my in-laws said that they would not attend the wedding if it took place in Portugal. I married in France to avoid such embarrassment.

After marrying, we moved into Paris from Sevres and lived in a hotel. I had a difficult pregnancy and could not work much. Even after my son was born I felt badly but we returned to Sevres and I began to work again for my old employer. Today I am still troubled by the pains and the malady I contracted then. I want to work hard, but sometimes I cannot.

My in-laws continued to write to my husband but they never mentioned me or sent me their best wishes. Then one day we heard that one of my sisters-in-law was making plans to be married. My parents-in-law invited my husband to come to the wedding. I told him that we should go to see what his family would do with me and with the baby. I arranged for someone to take over my job and we left; we arrived in Trancoso on a Saturday, market day, at Christmastime. We met two of my husband's sisters there and they said that my father-in-law was in the cafe. My husband went in and I remained outside, somewhat embarrassed. When they came out, my father-in-law came over to speak to me. He invited us to the house. We went and remained the night. We stayed longer with my in-laws than with my own parents and acted as godparents at the marriage. Today everyone gets along well but I will never forget the pain they caused me. In small villages, if people talk about a girl then the families of her boyfriends do not want their sons to marry her because it is shameful to them.

When we returned to France after my sister-in-law's wedding, I had lost my job. We spent more time than we had planned to in Portugal because there were problems with my passport. During that year, we moved several times because it was difficult to find a place to live. My sister at first talked with the manager of the "hotel" where she lived. He was nasty and told us the rent was higher than we thought it was. He would not give us a room. We went to stay in another hotel where it was prohibited to cook. My sister used to bring us meals so we would not have to eat out all the time. Later we found a room where we could cook and stayed there for a month. I was packing the suitcases on the last day to make yet another move to a larger place when who should arrive but my father-in-law and two of my sisters-in-law from Portugal. Thank goodness I already had a new room. We all slept there together. I bought a foam mattress to put on the floor. My sisters-in-law and I slept there and my husband shared a bed with his father on the other side of a curtain I had hung up to divide the room.

Soon my father-in-law and my sisters-in-law began to regret having left Portugal and my mother-in-law. We had trouble finding them work, especially the youngest who was only sixteen. My father-in-law became ill after six months and finally went back, but even today he regrets fleeing France so hastily because others now have more money that he does and now it is harder to arrange proper working papers than it was then. My sisters-in-law stayed, however, and today the youngest is already married. I had a lot of trouble with her at first because I felt responsible for her. She did not want to be chaperoned but I had to. After she was settled, we moved back into Paris. For a while, we lived in a studio apartment and paid rent. I could not work because of my sons, and soon it was apparent to us that the best thing would be to find a position as concierge. My eldest sister Julia was the one who found the place where we live now. When I first began working as a concierge, I also did a few hours of cleaning a day for some of the tenants in the building and made about 300 extra francs a month, which helped to supplement my husband's salary. The extra work tired me out so I stopped, and now devote myself to the duties involved in the concierge position. I find the work demanding. I cannot go out much because there are always people looking for me. If I am feeling ill and someone knocks on the door, I must get up to see what they want. In France, the life of an immigrant is one of work. There are some who enjoy life, who live exactly like the French, but the majority lead a life of sacrifice, eating badly and saving so that they can make a better life for themselves in Portugal in the future. On Sundays we stay home or visit with family. We have no other acquaintances. You cannot make friends with just anyone. I never had many friends in Portugal because they never keep secrets. My family is enough for me here.

Outside of my work, my greatest worry is my sons. I am giving them more or less the same education that I had. I always want to know where they are going because I am afraid that they will find companions who will lead them down the wrong paths. Parents can always watch their daughters more easily than their sons. I would like my sons to study so that they will have a life that is better than the one I have had, doing work that is cleaner than the work I have done. This is my greatest desire and for this reason I will stay in France for the moment. Someday, however, I will return to Portugal, even if my sons stay here. They will marry and have their own lives. If I had a daughter, perhaps it would be different. If she wanted me to live with her, I would like that. Daughters-in-law are something else however, and it is better to remain independent from them.

My enthusiasm for France is gone and I am already tired of the life here. I feel captivated because I am in a foreign country. There are many French people who do not like us to be here. There are foreigners, Portuguese and others, who come to France dirty and who are badly behaved. They rob us of all the respect that is due us. For this reason, I want to return to my own country some day. My husband is not so eager to return to Portugal as I am. He thinks the life is better in France, but that is because he only knew the life of the country in Portugal. My dream is to buy a house in the city in Portugal that we can rent. That way we will have some income. Then I will fix up the house and the land we have purchased in Seara and we can live there. If we cannot do this soon, we will do it when my husband retires. I will die there if I do not die here first.

I believe that every person has a destiny. But who arranged my marriage? It was not destiny. I married my husband because I came to France. My sister-in-law found her husband in France, too. Is that destiny? No. They are things we do ourselves. To explain what destiny is is impossible. Death is the destiny of us all. I do not know if it was my destiny to be in bad health. I only know that France has changed my life; but life in Portugal has changed too. Today they are building a chapel in my village. There was nothing there before. At one time they asked for contributions but the money was never quite enough. The idea was abandoned until the military men arrived in the summer of 1974 to view the situation. They want to put a new road in and they want to bring electricity. They want to create a new life there. Under Salazar the life in the countryside never changed. It was always backward. Today everyone wants change to happen right away. But patience is what we need.

When I die my sons can read about my life, about the sacrifices I have made and the suffering I have endured. France did well by me and for Portugal in general. If I had never left there I would be the same slave that I was before I left. But we never forget Portugal. Our memories despite our slavedom, are not bitter. We never forget the country where we are born, the village where we are raised, the past which is our own.

CHAPTER THREE

Second Story: Virginia Caldas

A minha vida não é um segredo
"My life is no secret"

Virginia Caldas was born in a larger, more accessible, and more economically diverse village in the district of Viana do Castelo in the northwestern province of Minho. Minho has frequently been referred to as the "garden of Portugal." The bright folkloric costumes of the women and the animated festivals have made this province famous in Portugal and abroad. Indeed, Virginia is the embodiment of the Minhotans, a Portuguese people known for their gaiety, hospitality, and deep-rooted Catholicism. The latter is best witnessed in the numerous pilgrimages (*romarias*) that the peasants of Minho undertake to nearby chapels and sometimes further south to Fatima where the Virgin is to have appeared before three shepherd children in the spring of 1917.

Minho is the homeland of *vinho verde*, the young wine that is heartily consumed by peasants throughout the province. The vines are trained up granite posts and along wires to form arbors that serve as markers to divide the small and haphazard plots of land that characterize this region of supreme *minifundia*. These arbors shade a lush and green landscape that carpets the hillsides and valleys of the province.

The village of Santa Eulalia is situated on the Lima river, one of the many rivers that cuts through Portugal flowing from the mountains in the interior towards the sea. The geography of the village is varied and includes a wide strip of wet marshland by the river's edge

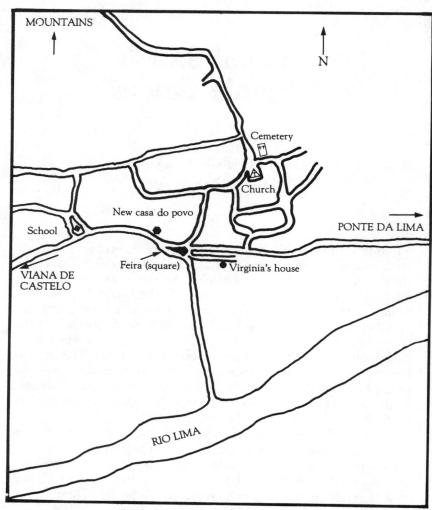

Map of the Village of Santa Eulalia

(the *veiga*)—perfect for the cultivation of corn, and mountainsides, where most village families own at least one plot of pine trees for fuel or for emergency cash. Like other Minhotan villages, Santa Eulalia is heavily affected today by emigration to France. According to the 1970 census, the population was 1,732 (815 men and 917 women) in 368 families and 454 households. The figure represents a 4 percent decline from 1960. This population is dispersed, residing in twenty neighborhoods (*lugares*) which cover approximately two square kilometers.

Santa Eulalia is a curious mixture of tradition and modernity. There are several old dwellings of both small and cut stones, some of them in the typical Minhotan style with two floors (the animals below and the people above) and a covered wooden verandah. Virginia's family home is of this type (see diagram in appendix) and consequently among the oldest houses in the village. There are also many new houses, the *casas francesas* as they are called, built by emigrants to France as symbols of their success abroad. These houses have enlivened the countryside of the province of Minho with bright colors and shiny facades of intricate tilework. They lend a modern air to the otherwise rustic landscape.

Most of the land in Santa Eulalia is divided into small parcels averaging one to three hectares (two and one-half to seven acres) in size. There are, however, a few larger farms of twenty-five hectares or more, some originally and still owned by enobled families, and others recently purchased by successful emigrants. The peasants of Santa Eulalia are subsistence farmers who cultivate a variety of crops. In addition to vines, they harvest corn, potatoes, cabbage, and olives. Between the rows of corn, beans and enormous squashes known as *abobora* are sown. After the corn is harvested in early September, the fields are planted with grass to provide winter pasture for the work animals.

Almost every family has a pair of oxen to work their fields. The wooden plow and the "roman" ox cart are still the major farming implements. Most families also raise barnyard animals: pigs, rabbits, chickens, ducks, and sometimes a milk cow. There is a milk depository on the outskirts of the village. The milk that is left there every morning and evening by young village women is taken to a regional factory and made into the local soft cheese.

There is one church in the village, recently restored with emi-

Virginia's aunt and sister-in-law shucking corn.

Virginia's paternal home.

grant contributions, and several small chapels dedicated to various saints. The church and the priest are still focal points of village life and religious participation remains strong. The patron saint's festival is celebrated in December and another major festa in July. Whereas Seara still had no electricity as late as 1975, Santa Eulalia has had electric light since the 1960s. There are also two school houses in the village, one a junior school constructed in the 1930s, and the other a more recent senior school located in the parochial building next to the church. These schools now serve the surrounding villages as well as Santa Eulalia. In addition to the schools, there is a new *casa do povo* (a community center and small clinic) built after the 1974 revolution to replace the old *casa do povo* on the village square. The village supports several small businesses, many of them owned by returned emigrants, and a gasoline pump which is manned by one of Virginia's brothers.

Virginia's description of life in Santa Eulalia presents a different portrait of the rural Portuguese family from that described by Ricardina. She was raised in a multigeneration household, living with her grandparents, parents and siblings, and her unwed aunts. Although such households are antithetical to the Portuguese aspiration expressed in the popular adage, *Quem casa, quer casa* ("whoever marries wants a house"),[1] they are common in some regions of Portugal—particularly the northeast, and are a solution to already extreme land parcellization in areas of high population density. Within such households, and Virginia's is an excellent example, the father or eldest male holds the reins of authority. For Virginia, searching for an alternative to this family situation in which she was raised, and for a life different from that which her mother had to endure as part of a larger household, became a major goal for emigration. By emigrating, she hoped to accumulate enough capital to build the *casa portuguesa* (or *casa francesa*) that her mother never had.

Virginia's discussion of family life is important in several other ways. She mentions, for example, three celibate aunts who are part of the multigeneration household she grew up in. High rates of celibacy, together with late ages at marriage, were common throughout western Europe in the latter nineteenth century and have been cited by numerous historical demographers as a means to limit population growth in the absence of more effective methods of birth control. Portugal, in particular, demonstrates significant levels of

Virginia's son, Joaquim, and his bride, 1978.

Virginia (far right) and her family in her mother's village. The photograph was taken during a Christmas visit, 1975.

female celibacy for at least a century, especially in the northern region. According to demographer Livi Bacci, the proportion of females who never married was as high as 22 percent in the latter part of the previous century and has declined slowly to 16 percent in 1960. Figures for Santa Eulalia show that Virginia's aunts are not alone in their celibate status (Table 6). These high rates of female celibacy have customarily been explained in connection with heavy male emigration which reduced the pool of potential husbands.[2] While male emigration would seem to play a very important role, in the case of Virginia's family a desire to keep the property intact (a logical motive for a household as prosperous as Virginia describes it) appears to have been more important in determining the celibate fate of several of Virginia's aunts.

TABLE 6:
Rates of Celibacy in Portugal, 1860–1960

	Percent Unmarried in Portugal, 50–54			Percent Celibate Deaths over fifty, Santa Eulalia	
Year	M	F	Period	M	F
1864	14.7[a]	21.7[a]	1860–69	10.0	33.9
1878	13.0[a]	20.2[a]	1870–79	11.9	33.3
1890	14.3	22.2	1880–89	11.6	18.2
1900	13.0	21.4	1890–99	8.2	24.3
1911	11.5	18.9	1900–09	9.3	33.8
1920	11.4	18.2	1910–19	6.5	28.2
1930	—	16.8	1920–29	4.5	37.5
1940	—	16.8	1930–39	6.3	32.8
1950	10.4	16.7	1940–49	6.4	29.6
1960	—	16.0	1950–59	15.2	31.2

a. 51–55 age group

Sources: Livi Bacci (1971) Table 8, p.40; vital registers, Santa Eulalia, 1860–1960

Virginia's discussion also alludes to the large size of Minhotan families until well into the present century. Her father was one of ten children, although only six survived to adulthood. Only in 1930 did the overall rate of fertility in Portugal begin to decline, and this decline came much more slowly in the northern half of the country than in the south. Clearly, large families placed enormous burdens upon the women of the rural north who had to juggle responsibilities of childcare with work in the fields. High fertility in the north has also been accompanied by high levels of infant mortality due, in large part, to poor systems of rural health care that only began to improve after the Second World War.

Although Virginia was unmarried at the time I interviewed her, she is the mother of an illegitimate son, born in 1954 when she was twenty-two. Despite the value placed upon virginity in Portugal, significant rates of illegitimacy have been characteristic since the late nineteenth century in northern Portugal, and locally, Santa Eulalia is no exception (Table 7).[3] Heavy male emigration, and the consequent disproportion of sexes, has been cited as an important cause of illegitimacy as well.

> Since a large fraction of the female population was forcibly excluded from marriage, it is not surprising to find a high number of illegitimate conceptions often tolerated by the family and the society.[4]

TABLE 7:
Illegitimacy Ratio,[a] Santa Eulalia, 1860–1960

Period	Proportion of Births Illegitimate	
	%	N
1860–69	11.4	31
1870–79	15.1	35
1880–89	10.1	24
1890–99	13.9	41
1900–09	13.9	43
1910–19	12.9	35
1920–29	9.5	31
1930–39	8.0	35
1940–49	3.6	16
1950–59	3.0	15

a. The illegitimate ratio is the proportion of illegitimate births among all births in a given period of time.

Source: vital registers, Santa Eulalia.

According to Virginia, an illegitimate birth brings shame (at least momentarily) upon a girl's family, but one mistake is generally forgiven. That a woman has an illegitimate baby is considered less unfortunate than the fact that she will find it difficult to catch a husband afterwards. Both civil laws and Church dogma favored the father, who could be compelled to affiliate and feed a child, but never to marry the mother. Indeed, parish birth registers consistently record the father and paternal grandparents as "unknown" despite the fact that parentage was often common knowledge. Even in cases where acknowledgement of responsibility by the father was imperative (when a girl was under eighteen), a young man had an option of marriage or prison. While figures do show that many illegitimate births were legitimated through subsequent marriage, many young men, like Virginia's suitor, chose emigration as an alternative. Virginia's personal saga concludes, in the Afterword to this book, with a reunion after twenty-four years of separation. The impact of emigration on Virginia's life, and on that of her cousin Mia, are symptomatic of the greater and more long-standing importance of male emigration in this region of Portugal in comparison with interior regions such as that from which Ricardina originates.

Virginia's attitudes towards marriage are perhaps a result of her own celibate status. She warns of the onerous burdens that marriage imposes upon Portuguese women by virtue of the accepted dominance of men and the double labors expected of women. Her portrayal of both her father and grandfather as authoritarian figures are clearly at the origin of this viewpoint and, certainly, influence her behavior toward her son's father as described in the Afterword. To this extent, her attitudes toward the ultimate authority of the male have changed less as a result of her experiences in France than have those of younger Portuguese migrant women who come to accept separation, at least ideologically, as a viable alternative to life with an over-demanding or abusive husband.

Virginia's descriptions of rural life are rich in ethnographic detail but, as is in keeping with her character, she chooses to relate some of the gayer aspects. Like Ricardina, she also had only minimal education and spent several years in domestic service. She is perhaps the most insightful in contrasting the experiences of a maid in Portugal and in France. Work of this nature in France is viewed as an infinite improvement because employers have more respect for their employees. Virginia's expressed attachment to her *patroa* is not at all uncommon among Portuguese women in France who find themselves working for a single family. While the relationship might appear paternalistic, for Portuguese migrant women it is flattery when they recall how servants are treated in Portugal.

Virginia emigrated to France when she was forty, but, like Ricardina, her final decision was motivated by social pressures and by disappointments and embarrassments in her personal life which made it impossible, from her point of view, either to remain in the village or return to her employer in Lisbon. Like other younger single Portuguese immigrant women, Virginia chose a position as a full-time maid for a bourgeois French family in the well-to-do Parisian suburb of Neuilly. Such a position offers not only economic security, but also security in housing. Her experience of relative job stability is, however, somewhat unique. One other woman of her age interviewed changed positions five times before finding one to her liking.

Virginia is the most religious of the three women whose stories are presented here. She contributes faithfully to her village church and, on occasion, has made *promessas* to give thanks for her own health or for that of someone close to her.[5] Of the three, she has the most active social life in France, revolving, in large part, about a local church where a Portuguese priest gives mass once a week. This Sunday community of immigrants is still rare among the Portuguese in the city of Paris; it probably flourishes in Neuilly because of the presence of a native priest and because of the high density of single Portuguese women who seek out the companionship of others to alleviate the relative isolation of their work experience.

It is through this church group that Virginia has had the opportunity to travel to such places as Lourdes, Rome, and England. Her attitude is that once she returns to Portugal, she will never again have the chance to see these tourist sites. Her age and single status allow her to spend her money more freely, and her personality is itself suited to some "enjoyment of life." Yet she is also serious in her plans for the future. Her goal of returning to Portugal appears to be both logical and resolute. She has no one to consider but herself and no family ties to influence her decision to remain. In this respect, she contrasts her own plans with those of her sister and brother-in-law. However, as the Afterword to this volume shows, life often throws snags in the carefully determined plans of the migrant.

My life is no secret. I was born in 1931, the third of four children. My mother's first child was a girl, but she died in her first year of life. They named my younger sister Rosa after her. I was named after my grandmother.

My grandfather died after my grandmother in 1951, at the age of eighty-eight. I remember him very well because he was always very strict with us when we were children. He had his own business, making and selling harnesses and other leather goods. He used to travel to the *feiras* ("markets") in Viana and Ponte de Lima to sell his things. We called him *pai de Viana* (father of Viana) for this reason. Before the busses came through Santa Eulalia, he used to travel in his horse and cart and he was gone all day. Viana seemed far away, though today one can get there in fifteen minutes in a car.

My grandfather was a good businessman; he made money and our house was abundant (*farta*). With this money he bought land and today our family owns plots throughout the village. We have also rented some plots for many, many years. For one we pay thirty-four rasas (thirteen kilograms) of corn per year. It is a large plot which used to be owned by some senhores, but which is now owned by two brothers who are emigrants in America.

My father was the eldest of ten children and the only surviving son. Many of his brothers and sisters had died even before my grandfather, two in 1918 when the Spanish flu took the lives of more than forty people in the village. When my grandfather died, he left all the land undivided and in my father's hands. It is unusual not to divide up the property (*fazer as partilhas*), but my grandfather did it that way because he wanted to make sure that my three unmarried aunts would be provided for, that my father would take care of them.

When I was growing up, we all lived in the same house together: my father, my mother, my brothers and sisters, my three aunts, my cousin, my grandfather and grandmother. There was another aunt, my father's youngest sister, but she married and then later died giving birth to her first child. My grandfather was very sad about that because he loved his youngest daughter very much.

My father, when he was small, learned to read and write, but he stopped school after two years to work in the fields. Only one of my aunts learned how to read, and not very well. People thought that it was a waste of time to send girls to school because they would not need their learning for anything. Whenever there was work to be done, especially at harvest time, the children simply missed school anyway. My father began to help my grandfather with his business when he was a young man and continued while we were growing up; but it was hard for him because he always had to obey my grandfather's orders. The business did well until tractors started coming into use and factories began to manufacture leather goods. The competition became too great and soon business was no longer profitable.

My father was practically born in the fields and there he died. One day, in the fall of 1968, he was out working after sundown and he fell from a tree. When he did not return for supper, my brother Manuel went out to look for him and found him lying in the fields unconscious. They called me to come from Lisbon where I was working. When I arrived and went to see him, he asked me who had sent for me. I told him that my sister Rosa had. He said "that is good." It was the last thing he ever said. He died four days after his fall at the age of seventy-two. My mother and my aunts have a special mass said for him every year in November, on the day he died. He, like my grandfather, left the land undivided in the hands of my oldest brother Joachim. This makes things complicated because no one knows what belongs to them. My brother refuses to go to the city hall to make the division because he does not want to have to pay the notary. It is a problem for me because I want to build a house there with the money I am earning in France, but I have to be sure that the land is mine before I start. Last summer we argued about this matter and I cried. My brother did not want to give me anything, and I am all alone except for my son.

My mother is seventy-seven years old. She was born to live and work the land. She comes from a village way up north, near the Spanish border. My father and mother were second cousins. My great-grandparents came originally from my mother's village to settle in Santa Eulalia and the family remained in contact although they did not see each other much. My father and mother met when my father was fulfilling his military service. He was stationed in the north and often went to visit with the family there. He fell in love with my mother when he first saw her, married her, and brought her to Santa Eulalia.

It was always difficult for my mother. She left her own family at the age of twenty-two and only went back once a year to visit. I remember those trips well. It took all day. My father and mother rode in the horse cart and we would run alongside. There were many hills to cross but we always enjoyed it because we saw new people and new places.

In Santa Eulalia my mother never had a house of her own. My father just built a new room onto my grandparents' house and everyone shared the same kitchen. Another room was added when my brothers and I were born. I always shared a bed with my sister and now when I return for vacation I share a bed with my mother. My mother worked all her life like a slave and had to do whatever her sisters-in-law (my aunts) and my grandmother wanted her to do because she was a stranger. My father never really understood the discomforts of her situation and she obeyed him in everything. Even today it is hard for her. She still works in the fields and sometimes she fetches water from the well eight times a day. She has some of her grandchildren there but the grandchildren she misses the most are my sister Rosa's children. They are all in France now. My son Carlos is with her but nowadays he talks constantly of emigrating to France or to Australia and that makes her cry. She has lived in that house for more than fifty years but she still feels like an outsider. In the old days, young couples rarely had enough money to build a house of their own like they do today, and once they were settled into the routine of living with others, they rarely moved.

I do not remember much about my childhood. I stopped going to school when I was ten years old because it was not obligatory to attend as it is today. I was having trouble in history and the teacher kept failing me. Finally I just quit and worked at home. Girls always work harder than boys. They have household chores (mending, cooking, feeding the animals) and help in the fields as well. My cousin Mia and I were always responsible for taking the cow and oxen to the fields to graze.

In the countryside, one day is much like another, but there are certain times of the year when there is special work to do. The time of year that we enjoyed the most as children was the wine harvest (*as vindimas*). Everyone was happy then; we would load the big wooden barrels onto the cart and take them up to the vines which were scattered on our land throughout the village. Sometimes we ate as many as we picked and returned in the evenings with purple mouths and purple fingers. It took days for the dye to wear off.

The grapes are left to ferment for a few days and then what wine there is is drained off so that the rest of the fruit can be transferred to the press. In the past, they used to press grapes with their feet, but for as long as I can remember, we have had a press of granite and wood in the back of the house. Sometimes there were good years and sometimes there were bad years, but there was usually always enough wine to last a year. The new wine is left to ferment in kegs for a month and then on 11 November, Saint Martin's day, it is opened up to drink. The skins and seeds of the wine are taken to the still and made into brandy (*aguardente*). The men drink this brandy in the morning with their coffee to "kill the beast" (*matar o bicho*— "warm the soul").

Much of the agricultural work has changed now. In the past even the corn harvest was a gay time. Families would gather together to husk the corn, singing and joking as they worked. If anyone found an ear of red corn they could kiss everyone present. Everyone grows corn in my village. It is used to make bread and to feed the animals. Nowadays, however, only a few families continue to bake bread with corn because there is a bakery that makes wheat bread every day and people prefer that.

The other festive occasions I remember are the pig killings, Christmas and Easter. I have not seen a pig killing for many years now, but it is still very important for every family. There were mornings in late November and December when you could hear the screams of a dying pig from one corner of the village to the other. There are men in the village whom you call to slaughter the pig, but in our family we always did it ourselves. My brother Manuel still acts as *matador*.

Everyone becomes involved, even the children. On the first day, after breakfast, you move the pig out into the yard and place it on a cart. It takes about five people to hold it down. Everyone is nervous and frightened because there are stories of pigs who escape with the knives still in their throats. It is important to put the knife in at just the right place so that all the blood will flow out into a bowl that one of the women holds on the ground under the pig's throat. She must stir the blood continuously so that it will not congeal before cooling. When the pig is dead it is placed on a piece of metal on the ground and fire is set to it so as to burn the hair off. The men do this, working fast to scrape off the hair from the blackened corpse.

When that is finished the pig is washed with soap and water until it turns a nice golden color. By that time, the body is slightly bloated and very stiff. The next step is to cut open and clean out the insides. There was a game that we used to play as children whenever a female pig was killed. My father would cut off the teats and we would try to sneak them into each other's pockets.

The intestines are saved and put aside because during the afternoon the women take them to the river to wash them out. They are precious as sausage casings. The liver, kidney, lungs, and heart are transported to the kitchen where the woman of the house prepares them, with rice and a bit of blood, into the traditional dish served at pig killings, *sarrabulho*. When the pig is totally cleaned, it is hung up to dry out for a day and everyone goes to eat. The meal is plentiful, as is the one on the following day when the carcass is cut up. That day was one of the few times a year that people in the village had fresh pork to eat. Fresh meat was always very special. Today families often kill a chicken or a rabbit every Sunday, but when we were small we only had chicken at Christmas or Easter.

These are the memories I have of my village and of my childhood. There was always lots of work, but also times for celebration. I used to enjoy the summer festas most because people who are sad and miserable most of the year are always happy and gay on these days. It is this gaiety that I miss the most now that I am living in France.

When I was eighteen I went to work for a rich family in Lisbon. In Santa Eulalia there is an enobled family; they are counts and countesses and they own a manor house (*solar*) in the village. They own a lot of land and have many laborers (*caseiros*) working for them. They used to spend their summers in the village but they lived the rest of the year in their big house in Lisbon. I remember when the son of the old count (who is now dead) was married. All the villagers were invited to the house for the wedding feast. His wife is from another noble family that has a home further up the river.

My father did not want me to go to work as a maid; we had enough money, he said, and I did not need to work. But I wanted to go and since my father knew the Senhor Conde he decided to let me. I worked for them for three years, spending nine months in Lisbon and three in the village. Sometimes the Condes also returned to Santa Eulalia for Christmas.

I worked very hard in Lisbon. The only time I had to myself was between four in the afternoon and eight in the evening on Sundays, but if I had not attended church in the morning, I always went then. My major duty was to serve tables. There were three maids in the house and we all slept together in one room. Being a maid in Portugal is very different from serving in France. In France you are freer, more independent. You even have your own room. In Portugal you have to be on your knees all the time. Otherwise they do not think you are working. In France there are machines to do that kind of work and if I am not feeling well my *patroa* lets me lie down to rest. When I had my operation last year, my *patroa* had to pay me even though I did not work.[6] In Portugal, if I were sick, I would be fired and someone else would replace me. There were always many girls looking for work. Serving was the only job available to girls who wanted to leave the fields.

I stayed in Lisbon for three years. Then, one of the other maids in the house became pregnant and the "condessa" was afraid that I might too. She did not want that kind of responsibility and sent me back to Santa Eulalia. But it was when I was back in the village that I "arranged my baby."

My son's father was a boy from the next village. I met him at a festa. He began to talk with men and later we became *namorados*. He was so good looking that I was crazy about him. He would write me letters that he sent through his sister who worked in the milk depository. I had to go there every day with our milk so I always received them. Other times he would follow me to the mines where I went to bring lunch to my brother. When a young man in Portugal is interested in a girl he will even leave his work to follow her. Often I took different routes just to avoid him. But a woman is weak, especially for a young man and soon it is impossible to say no anymore. I started to meet him secretly. I used to tell my father that I was going to my cousin's home to help her write letters (she did not know how to write herself) and then I would meet him instead. It was in this way that the baby came. I trusted and believed him when he said he would marry me. If I had not, I would never have let him go as far as he did. I did it the first time to experiment without a good idea of the consequences.

"What do you want me to do about it," he said to me when I told him that I was pregnant. He wanted me to get rid of the child in Viana, but I refused. My father was very angry with me, but he finally accepted it and did not throw me out of the house. There were other girls in similar situations, three others that same year in my village. One mistake is usually forgiven; but more than one, rarely. Besides, one of my father's sisters also had a baby out of wedlock (my cousin Mia). My aunt wanted her to marry the man, but my grandfather refused because he did not think the man was good enough for her and thought that she would be better off at home. My grandfather was a man like that, very proud.

My own baby was born in April 1954. After his birth, I stayed in my father's house. The condessa wanted me to return to work for her (maybe she thought that after I had had a child there would be less risk of having another), but I did not want to work while my baby was still so young. My son's father went off to Lisbon to work. Once he came back to Santa Eulalia for a visit and sent me a note asking me to meet him with the baby. I went, but my father followed me that time because he did not want the shame of another child. He need not have worried, because I knew better and would never have let it happen.

My son's father finally began to arrange the papers for our marriage. Then his uncle wrote to him from Venezuela, urging him to emigrate. He changed his mind about marrying me and left. Before he went away he came to our house and promised my mother that he would marry me someday, but only when he had enough money so that I would not have to work like a slave. He wrote from every point where the ship stopped. He went to Venezuela first and then to Brazil. From time to time he sent money, saying that he wanted his son to be educated and well dressed. But he never returned, even when I wrote to tell him that his own father was dying. He continued to write to me and to my son until 1973. Then the letters stopped. Even his sisters have not heard from him.

There are many women in Portugal, married and unmarried, who are in similar situations. My cousin Mia, for example, married in 1952 and a month later her husband departed for Brazil, leaving her behind. Everyone thinks that the fellow married her for her looks, not for love. She was the prettiest girl in the village. Mia waited for six years before her husband called her to join him in Brazil. She spent about eight months there, but she could not tolerate the heat and returned to Santa Eulalia in the fall of 1958. By that time she was pregnant. Her daughter is a young woman, but she has never seen her father and my cousin has now lost touch with her husband. But some day he might return. If he does it will be hard for her to adjust because she has been so self-sufficient and independent for so many years. In one sense he has ruined her life because she is not free to marry or to go anywhere. She wanted to emigrate to France too, to make money, but in order to go legally she needed to have her husband's permission and he was not around to give it.

When my son was three years old, I decided to return to Lisbon to work. I left him with my mother and father. All I thought about was making a life for him, seeing that he had everything he needed. I never once looked at another man, though other women in my position might have. Once, another man proposed to me, but I wanted to marry my son's father or no one because another man might not love my son as his own. My life continued in this way until my son was fourteen years old. He had been studying in the village school and in the school in Viana. He was a bright student, but he was lazy. Finally he wrote asking me if he could come to Lisbon to live me and I agreed. I found him a job in an office and he began to work.

It was about that time that I was writing to my son's father to ask him to send the proper papers so that my son could take his father's name as well as mine. I mentioned it in every letter, but he never sent the documents. One day they arrived and I took them to the city hall. It was then that I discovered that he had married someone else without telling me, a Brazilian woman. I cried and cried, but at least my son was finally able to take his father's name.

Two years passed until my son's father wrote again calling us to Brazil to join him. He wrote that his brother was returning to Portugal on a trip and that he would bring us back with him. He said that the other woman had left him. I was so crazy about him (he was the first man I knew) that I dropped everything. I quit my job in Lisbon and returned to the village to make preparations for our departure. I even bought a new dress to wear when I arrived. I was very happy because my dream of marrying him was finally coming true. However, at the last moment, the Portuguese government would not give my son a passport because he was sixteen and approaching the age for military service. I could not go without my son. I was heartbroken, ashamed, and without work.

By that time, my younger sister was married and had four small children. Her husband, my brother-in-law, had been in France for several years along with many others from Santa Eulalia. He became sick because he was not eating properly and wrote to ask my sister to join him. She did not want to leave the village but felt that it was her duty to join her husband. She began to try to convince me to go with her, saying that I was a good worker and could find employment easily in France. I had so much experience as a maid and that was the kind of work that was available to Portuguese women in France. I told her that I would go only if I had a contract because I was afraid of the *salto* ("clandestine emigration") and afraid to go to France as a single woman. But I really had no other alternative. Finally she persuaded me to go. We left with tourist visas. My sister's children remained with my mother and my cousin. We arrived in France in October 1971.

And so, at the age of forty, I started a new life for myself on foreign soil. In France, it was not hard for me to secure the proper papers. I arrived on a Saturday in October, and by the following Monday I had already found work through a friend, another woman from Santa Eulalia. I have worked for the same *patroa* since the beginning. I earn fourteen hundred francs (approx $300) a month plus room and board. The salary is so much greater than the 150 escudos (approx six dollars) a month I earned in Lisbon. I send most of my money back to Portugal because, with my room and board paid for, I have little need to spend much here. My brother Joachim takes care of it for me in a bank there. Perhaps if I were younger I would want to buy new clothes and such but now the most important thing for me is to save so that some day I can build a little house for myself in the village. I have not been able to save very much yet because of my son. He always wants things and I cannot refuse him. Last year he bought a motorbike. He was in the army a short time but was finally excused because of an old knee injury that he got once playing *futébol*. When he was in the army he took a room in a hotel with a friend and I ended up paying for that too. He thinks he is a *fidalgo* and I know that I am partly responsible for that because I spoil him. But I cannot help it; I want him to have everything that I did not have.

I do not want to stay in France all my life. When I have saved enough, I will build a house in Santa Eulalia for myself and my son. It will have two floors so that I can live on one and my son and his family (when he marries and has a family) can live on the other. The house where my mother and aunts live is old and crowded and my son dislikes living there. The old ladies argue with one another. In our own house we could live in peace, independently. It is not my family that pulls me back to the village, but the ambience of village life; it is gay and everyone knows one another. Young people leave there because life in the countryside has no future, it gives nothing. But I am not starting life like they are; for me life is almost over and I have already worked hard enough. I will have a little garden next to my house, but I will never work in the fields. By the time I retire my son will have a job and he can help me as I have helped him. The only thing that worries me is that my son will emigrate to France, or somewhere else, because then I will be all alone.

My sister does not really want to stay in France either. She, like I, does not speak any French and consequently spends most of her time at home. Her husband, however, has no wish to return to Portugal. He feels that he can give his children a better life in France. The youngest hardly speaks Portuguese. Unlike my sister, I have neither husband nor children to tie me down like that. I can make decisions on my own. I value my independence. To me it means that I do not have to ask anyone for help. I work and can make a life for myself and my son. I have no regrets about never having married. Sometimes a girl thinks that throughout her life each day will be like the day she married. But that is not so. You lose some of your independence when you marry, you are "taken" by someone. After you are married, if you want to go somewhere but your husband does not want to go then you cannot go. In Portugal it used to be that once a boy and a girl became *namorados*, the boy would begin to order the girl around. Now things are changing a little and both have more freedom. But I still believe in many of our old sayings:

> *Antes que cases, vê o que fazes*
>
> "Before you marry, watch what you are doing"
>
> *Solteirinha não te cases. Goza-te de boa vontade*[7]
>
> "Single one do not marry. Enjoy yourself at will"

A lot of things are changing in Portugal as a result of emigration. Everyone has money now. Marriages and baptisms are something to be seen. Many girls come to France to earn money so that they can arrange a trousseau for themselves. They can marry more easily if they have money, clothes, perhaps even a house. Sometimes they marry men they meet here and other times, they marry an old *namorado* from the village. But even if they meet their future husband in France, most go back to celebrate the marriage there. They invite the entire village, and especially the emigrants. The importance of a wedding is now measured by the number of cars there are in the procession. The emigrants are invited because they give good presents; they are "rich" and they want to show off. When I was younger, I was never invited to weddings because I was not wealthy. But now, oh, la, la! I try to avoid going to too many because then my money would all be spent. Last summer my cousin's child asked me to be the godmother at her wedding. I had to buy a new dress and a nice present. The wedding feast was held in a hotel in Viana instead of in the bride's home as it used to be in the past.

I spend most of my time working in France but every summer I go back to Portugal for a month. I know several other Portuguese immigrants in France through the church. There is a Portuguese mass every Sunday, given by a young Portuguese priest. He is studying in Paris, but he has also been appointed to our church to say the mass and help us with our problems. Couples come from all over the city to be married by him. Sometimes there are festas in the church organized by the younger girls who live in the area. Last year they put on a religious play and danced some of the village dances of Portugal. A few years ago I travelled to Rome with a group from the church and I have been to Lourdes three times. I like to see things and now I have the money to pay for these trips. My *patroa* is always very understanding and gives me the time off. One weekend I also went on a religious retreat with the younger girls. I was worried about it at first because I am so much older and have had a son. But the priest told me that it was perfectly all right for me to attend.

Sometimes I see people from the church on Sunday afternoons, but usually I visit with my sister and her family. I leave after mass and spend the rest of the day with them. I know how to travel to her house on the bus. I also visit with her on Thursdays when I have my afternoon off. My only other friend here is a woman who lives just across the river. She is from the village but I never knew her as a friend when I was growing up. It is only in France that we have become friendly. When I do not go to my sister's I go there. Her husband has been very good to me and helps me out when I have a problem. The other day he went with me to help resolve a legal matter. In the village if people had seen me alone with him who knows what they might have said. You cannot claim a married man as your friend there. People immediately suspect something else.

Other than these visits, I do not get around Paris much. I work from seven in the morning until eight or nine at night. I have two hours of rest at midday but there is always work to do. My *patroa* does the shopping but I do all the cooking. She teaches me how to make a dish once and then I can remember for the next time. But they usually eat very simply. I serve them at table. The only time that things become complicated is when they have guests. I finish my work late but I do not mind because I like to spend as little time as possible in my room. It is sad there when I am all alone.

I have no regrets about coming to France. I have been able to see new places and to do things that I could never have done if I remained in Portugal. I know that I will not be here forever and that makes it possible for me to stay just a little longer. Some women complain about their *patroas* and that makes life more difficult for them here. But I have been lucky. If I had not found an understanding *patroa* I might not have stayed as long as I have. I count my blessings. Things have gone well, *graças a deus*.

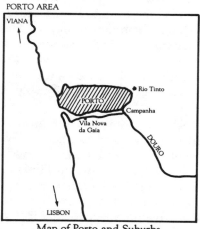

Map of Porto and Suburbs

CHAPTER FOUR

Third Story:
Ana Fernandes

Não há dinheiro nenhum que paga a ausencia da familia
"No amount of money can make up for
the absence of one's family"

Ana Fernandes was born in 1943 in Campanha, a working-class sprawl of the city of Porto, Portugal's second largest city and the important port city of the north. Porto is built up on the craggy right bank of the Douro river, not far from the Atlantic Ocean. Across the river is the city of Vila Nova da Gaia where the grapes from the upper Douro valley are made into the famous Port wine.

Porto is a business city, more sombre, and perhaps more bourgeois than the nation's capital. It was in Porto that the *brasileiros*, the "nouveaux riches" emigrants who managed to return from Brazil with some of their newly found wealth, built some of their more splendid mansions in the late nineteenth and early twentieth centuries—mansions that the social realist writer Julio Dinis has described so well in his novel *Uma Familia Inglesa*.

> The eastern section [of Porto] is mainly Brazilian since it is there that the capitalists from America gather. Huge granite masses, little palaces, predominate; a large gate, tiled walls, the rooves with blue eaves, the verandahs blue and gold, the gardens geometrically laid out and with stairways adorned with china statues. . . . The houses abound with gothic windows and rectangular doors, rectangular windows and gothic doors. In the window, almost always, there is the face of an indolent capitalist.[1]

Along the Avenida dos Aliados at the heart of the city one finds those who are perhaps the descendants of these brasileiros—well-

Ana Fernandes with her husband Domingos and her two daughters.

Ana Fernandes, July 1980.

dressed bankers, businessmen, and bourgeois housewives sitting in tea shops and cafes watching people spill out of São Bento station nearby. The city is alive with conversation and activity.

Porto is also an industrial city and the center of one of the most important economic areas in the country. The major industries are textiles (cotton), metallurgy, chemicals, food canning, leather goods, and ceramic production. Four miles away, in the small town of Gondomar, one also finds the craftsmen who make the filligree gold jewelry that adorns even peasant women on special feast days. It is these industries that employ about one-third of the working-class population of the city, a population which has been growing steadily in the last several decades.

Densely populated, Porto has a large sector of poorly housed and poorly fed families. It is not uncommon to see barefooted women selling wares on street corners, or children begging for an escudo here and there. The narrow, twisted streets built up to and around the hilltop cathedral make no pretense of hiding the misery along them. Many families still live crowded into one room with no running water and no place to throw their waste but onto the streets. France clearly offered a brighter future to these tenement dwellers, and increasingly, during the latter 1960s, these people filled the ranks of Portuguese nationals emigrating to France.

As in the rural areas, the men frequently emigrated first, leaving their wives to replace them in the factories. Unlike their rural counterparts, however, they often left with no contacts in the country to which they were emigrating. Perhaps their experiences in a metropolitan environment made it easier for them to deal with the new, though foreign, context. It was not the first time that they had worked in a factory or ridden on a bus or train, as it was for many emigrants from strictly peasant backgrounds.

Ana and her husband Domingos, like many other *portuenses*, found their way to France at the end of the decade of the 1960s after the massive exodus from rural Portugal was well under way. At the time of my acquaintance with them, they were living in a little two-story cottage in a suburb north of the city of Paris and paying five hundred francs a month in rent. Ana seemed to be quite proud of this little house which she said she kept in good order so that if her mother came to visit she would see that Ana and Domingos lived in "satisfactory conditions."

On the ground floor there is a small living room furnished with a formica-topped table, a large buffet, an overstuffed chair, and a television. On top of the buffet and the table are pieces of crochet work that Ana has made. The small toilet and kitchen complete the ground floor. Upstairs are two bedrooms, each furnished with a bed and a large *armoire*, and a bathroom. Outside, Ana and Domingos have a garden planted with a few potatoes and cabbages. Although Ana is very proud of this small home, they have submitted an application to the city hall for public housing, but until they bring their children to France to join them, there is little chance of securing this form of shelter.[2] The waiting list for public housing is very long. In the meantime, however, they are comfortably settled and both hold down steady jobs, Ana as a member of the cleaning staff of the local clinic, and Domingos as a solderer for a construction firm.

While Ana did not recount much of her childhood, she does leave us with some impressions of the piecemeal way of life of Portuguese urban working-class women who, because of their husbands' low salaries and large families, are forced to go out themselves and earn a living in whatever way they can.[3] Maria Lamas, in her book, *As Mulheres do Meu Pais*, published in 1948, has written about the entire gamut of occupations (breadsellers, washerwomen, fishmongers, etc.) filled by these women. Many of these activities are not adequately represented in Portuguese female labor statistics and therefore lead to an underestimation of the significant economic contributions made by working-class wives to the upkeep of the family.

The growth of the textile industry in the Porto-Guimarães-Familicão triangle after the Second World War made it possible for women of Ana's generation to find alternatives and less piecemeal employment. Throughout Portugal, the textile industry employed 67 percent of the active female population in the secondary sector in 1950, 65 percent in 1960, and 62 percent in 1970. Until 1974, the salaries for women were roughly half those paid to men in all sectors of activity. In addition to their salaried employment, working-class women, as Ana notes, continue to have all the responsibilities of childcare and spend most of their Sundays engrossed in household chores.[4]

The Portuguese female labor force is characterized by its youth and is symptomatic of the tendency of young girls to leave school at an early age. Ana herself began to work in a textile factory at the age of thirteen. Portuguese labor laws governing the employment of minors were not rigorously enforced and even permitted children of primary-school age to engage in remunerated work in domestic service or in agriculture. Indeed, the enforcement of child labor laws would probably have been extremely unpopular among the lower classes of Portuguese society, who needed the meagre salaries of as many able hands as possible to keep themselves afloat.

The circumstances behind Ana Fernandes's emigration were somewhat different from those of Ricardina and Virginia because she was already married and had two children. Although her husband's emigration could be called as spur-of-the-moment as that of Ricardina or Virginia, Ana emigrated more out of a sense of duty than of freedom and new beginning. Indeed, the majority of Portuguese women in France have entered that country as part of a process of familial regroupment. While some of these women (like Virginia's sister Rosa) emigrated with their children or had every intention of bringing them to France soon after their own arrival, Ana decided quite firmly to leave her children behind in the care of her mother so that she could work full-time in France, thereby contributing more completely to the accumulation of funds and to the achievement of the ultimate goal of returning to Portugal as soon as possible. This pattern of migration is by no means uncommon among Portuguese couples in France and is equally characteristic of other southern European migrants in northern Europe (for example, Turkish women in Germany; see Kudat, 1975). It distinguishes the intra-European population flow from many other trans-Atlantic migrations where married female migration implied familial migration. Ana points quite definitely to the problems resulting from this pattern of migration. Children grow up knowing only their grandmothers as mothers and feeling alienated from parents they see only once a year. For many Portuguese women in France, this represents a real personal crisis.

The important aspect of Ana's story is that it also presents the deliberations that ensue as the time spent abroad becomes longer and longer. Among similar couples interviewed in France, Ana and Domingos were the only ones who had, in fact, attempted a definitive return. Their consequent reemigration is the fate one would expect for many potential returnees, although in their case returning to an urban employment structure was perhaps more difficult, economically speaking, than returning to set up a small business in a rural environment. The latter has been achieved by a small minority of Portuguese emigrants who have reinstalled themselves in their native villages after many years in France, although these are, for the most part, men who emigrated alone.

At several points in the narrative, we are able to compare, through Ana's eyes, aspects of the way of life and values of the urban working class with those of the peasantry. The most outstanding similarity emerges in her discussion of courtship. Of the three women, Ana is the most vocal in her emphasis upon male authority and sexual purity. Her more deliberate support of virginity might be accounted for by the Victorian morality of bourgeois and upper-class lifestyles and values to which she has had greater exposure. The comment that Ana makes about the rather oblique way in which she learned about sex is indicative of the fact that Portuguese mothers, urban and rural, rarely tell their daughters about the "facts of life." It is this relative lack of knowledge that frequently leads to "mistakes."

Ana probably offered the most insightful interpretation of the nature of male dominance in Portuguese society. She cites an adage that several Portuguese migrant women used to explain male authority and the separate spheres of influence for men and women:

> *Em casa manda ela; mas nela mando eu*
> In the home she rules; but I rule her.

Although many social scientists have recently claimed the influence that women have in the domestic sphere as a source of "real" power[5]—the old "behind every man there is a woman" theory, in Portugal, if we are to believe Ana's interpretation, there is clearly a difference—a difference defined not only by certain structural conditions, but also ideologically. The phrase *em casa manda ela; mas nela mando eu* embodies this ideological difference, although, as Ana points out, it does not contradict a certain economic equality in conjugal relations among Portuguese rural and urban working-class couples. To some extent, Ana's remarks on male dominance reflect a period of transition. "Many women," she says, "are afraid to assert themselves. They are not aware of their rights." Given the relative lack of rights that Portuguese laws accorded to women until quite recently, Ana's comments are clearly a result of her exposure to the French way of life and French legislation. Nevertheless she is quite vocal in her distaste for male-female relations among the bourgeoisie of France. She simply has no place for the well-to-do French woman who spends her day in leisure time activities and who exploits the labors of her husband. A similar point of view is expressed by other Portuguese women in France. Ana's expectations for herself are hard-nosed and realistic in comparison with Ricardina. She will never be "just a housewife," but will always work to help her husband support the family.

For Ana, the greatest benefit in emigrating to France has been the changes that it has brought about in her husband. He has matured and they share more experiences together. Unlike Ricardina and Virginia, Ana and Domingos have no family in France and consequently have found a few compatriots whom they consider as friends. However, Ana draws a connection between "money and friends" that is almost brutal in its frankness. In the long run, she is cautious about her associations with other Portuguese. This is an attitude expressed frequently by immigrants who have been raised, for the most part, in communities where everyone knows one another. As one other migrant woman put it,

> We all come from different parts of Portugal. People tell you about themselves, but how do you know if it is true? You have to be careful. You can't just be friendly with everyone.

This predominant feeling of distrust for anyone with whom you have not "grown up with" and whose background you are not familiar with has its origins in several incidents of exploitation of Portuguese by Portuguese, especially during the early years of emigration to France. In the bidonvilles, for example, those who had been in France longer charged newcomers for certain services, playing upon their ignorance. They often exacted high rents for tin can shelters that they had built for nothing. Ana's own story of the woman who cheated her on rent money is another example. She explains this exploitation as a result of a form of competitiveness that has emerged among the Portuguese in France, a competitiveness that she claims did not exist in urban Porto where everyone lived in equal misery. This is somewhat different from the portrait of rural Portugal presented by Ricardina and might be explained by the more destitute and hopeless conditions of the urban poor. This sense of hopelessness, of fate, is expressed in Ana's final comments. In a way that is both simple and profound, she describes the limbo in which many migrants live.

My mother was one of eight children. Her father was a "gypsy." He used to go off for long stretches of time, buying and selling animals, leaving my grandmother alone to cope as best she could. I hardly remember him because he died when I was two years old. My grandmother eventually went crazy and spent a lot of time in the hospital. She would break things and rave madly, but she never did anything to harm us.

My mother left home when she was sixteen and went to live with another elderly couple. In order to earn her keep, she used to sell fruit and vegetables which she carried on her head in a big basket from door to door. She met my father in Rio Tinto,[6] and only after they were married did they move to Campanha, where I was born. My father worked as a solderer in a factory all of his life. It is from his family that we inherited the nickname of *canastra* ("basket"). His ancestors were basket weavers. Even today, people know my children as the daughters of Ana Canastra rather than as the daughters of Ana Fernandes.

When my brothers and sisters and I were small, my mother stopped her selling, but she still took in laundry and sewing in her spare time. She always had some kind of extra work. Women in Portugal have to help out because what the man earns is never enough to support the family. As soon as I was old enough to take care of my younger brothers and sister, she became a breadseller. She would go out between five and nine in the morning and again in the evenings, selling small loaves from door to door. "Bread, sirs, for the love of God. Give me a penny to buy milk for the baby," that is what all the women used to cry.

In Portugal, there are four classes—the rich, the middle, the poor, and the miserable. Many people in Porto are in the miserable class, very, very poor. They go to buy things in a place, pay for it and then the next time return to establish credit. They buy on credit until it is cut off because the bill is too high and they cannot pay it. Then they go somewhere else and start all over again. They borrow and beg wherever they can.

I went to school for four years and then my mother took me out and sent me to a seamstress to learn how to sew. At first, my mother paid twenty-five escudos a month, but the seamstress soon realized that she could hardly afford it so she gave me cleaning to do as well as sewing tasks. I stayed there for three years and then, at the age of thirteen, I went to work in an umbrella factory. Until I was married,

I always gave my salary to my mother. She would put some of it aside for me, or buy things for my trousseau and then use the rest for the family. Young girls in France spend everything they earn and then, when it comes time to get married, they have nothing. In Portugal, girls are better prepared; instead of going out at night, they spend their time sewing and embroidering. It costs less to embroider sheets yourself and you can do it to your liking. Keeping girls at this work is also a way to supervise them.

My mother was constantly watching over me. When I needed to go out on an errand, she would follow me because she was afraid that I would begin talking to some boy and then get into trouble. At first, I did not realize that she was there, but once I found out, I sometimes took alternate routes to lose her. I wanted to be in peace with the young men, although I would never have done anything. I remember once when I was walking home from the factory with a girlfriend of mine who was seventeen and her boyfriend who was nineteen. My girlfriend went off and left me to walk the rest of the way with the boy. I was afraid, not only of him, but also of what my parents would do if they saw me. They always assume the worst, because if a girl does get pregnant, it is shameful to her parents.

However, I think it is good that they were watchful and I will do the same with my children because I want them to be able to say on their wedding night as I said: "This is the first time that I am sleeping with a man." I want them to be married in white as I was. Men can tell if their wives are not virgins and a girl who has lost her virginity will have a hard time finding a husband. A man always tries to get as much as he can from a girl and the girl who refuses him will be the one to get him in the end because she will have his respect. If a girl lets him go ahead, then once he has had her, he will go on. We have a saying that when a dog sees a bone he begins to chew on it. But then if someone offers him another, he will drop the first for the second.

A girl should tell a man who wants to marry her if she has lost her virginity. Then, seeing that she is honest, he may still marry her. If he has to find out on his own, he will surely be angry. And there are always people to tell him. Most often it is other girls who are jealous who will let him know. The tongues are always wagging. There was one young man in our neighborhood who refused to marry a girl he had got into trouble. He went to prison instead. Another man joined him in prison one day and they began to talk. The second man told of a girl who had refused to marry him, or have anything to do with other men until the father of her child had married someone else. It turned out to be the same girl and when the young man was free, he married the girl because she was honorable.

No one ever talked much about me because I had only one serious boyfriend before my husband. My husband lived on the same street as I. He was the nicest looking boy around, but he was always dressed so poorly. His father, who was a clogmaker, died when he was two and a half. His mother remarried and had another child. She did not love my husband so he was raised by his aunt. I hated to see him suffering and I began to watch after him in a way. I washed his clothes and looked after his best interests. My parents were against our marriage because he had never proven to be any good. He had never worked seriously and was lazy, but I did marry him in 1961 when I was only nineteen. Then the troubles began.

We moved in to live with his aunt. He finally found work in the same factory where my father worked, but soon after he began to miss days or arrive late. Meanwhile, I continued to work in the same factory where I worked before marrying. My sister and step-sister also had jobs there. Sometimes I arose at four in the morning in order to finish all the household chores before setting out to work. I worked like a slave to be at the factory by seven in the morning.

In March of 1962, my husband went into the military for twenty-eight months. He was stationed in Porto because he was married. It was in April of that year that I discovered that I was pregnant. But the baby died right after it was born. Time passed and two more children were born. They lived.

My husband picked up all kinds of bad habits in the military. Although he never looked at other women, he used to go out nights with a couple of friends to taverns to drink and spend money. I had to scrimp and save in order to keep the little ones fed. My husband did not want me to work, but I had to. My mother was a saint. She watched the children during the day. Sometimes she would interfere when my husband came home drunk or angry and began to beat me. Once he even broke one of her fingers. Many times I wanted to kill myself because I was so unhappy, but I had the children to consider. They were often sick and needed to be cared for.

Life went on like that for several years. Then one night, after my husband was out of the military but without a job, he decided to emigrate to France to make money. He wanted me to go with him, but I refused, so he planned to go with some friends clandestinely. He pawned some of my things to raise money for the passage. He also borrowed money from some people, telling them that it was for one of his children who was very sick. I had to pay that money back after he left. He was always getting himself into trouble where money was concerned. In fact, just before he decided to go he had been accused of stealing some money from the funds of an informal club to which he belonged with his friends. When I discovered the accusations, I begged him to tell me the truth. He denied stealing the money but was very upset about the fact that someone thought him a thief. Better to leave than to live down a reputation. That was what he was thinking. He would have to make a go of it in France, for to return a failure would have been even more shameful.

He left for France in September 1969. He wrote often and I cried every time I read a letter. He lived for a while in a room with several Algerians, found factory work, and even sent some money home. But then he became sick and wrote asking me to join him there. He said that he could not survive without me, that he did not know how to cope on his own. He returned at Christmas time as a surprise and I was very glad to see him. I forgot all the misery he had caused me. He borrowed money from my father to return to France in the New Year, but not before I had promised him that I would go with him to France at Easter time. I decided to leave the children behind with my mother since I did not know what was awaiting me abroad. I will always remember the girls in the factory talking about France, about how you could make a lot of money there. But I never thought that I would go. Then all of a sudden, I found myself involved in the same adventure, the same dream of many Portuguese.

When I arrived in France, we had no decent place to live but we soon found a room in the attic of a house that a Portuguese couple was renting. The Portuguese woman told me that she paid three hundred francs (sixty dollars) a month and that we could split the cost with her. I found work cleaning for the French family who owned the house. The Portuguese woman told her that I was a cousin. I also found other hours of work by putting up a notice in the local bakery. Soon I was earning five hundred francs a month. I sent most of the money to my mother for the children. How I missed them.

I was very pleased with myself until one day, talking to the French lady who owned our house, I mentioned in my broken French that we were paying one hundred and fifty francs (thirty dollars) rent for the attic. The French lady became very angry, telling me that that was all she charged the Portuguese women for the whole house. So my husband and I were paying the entire rent of the other family. She went to speak with the other Portuguese woman who became mad at me and cut off electricity and water in the attic. Then one night we found ourselves locked out and had to sleep in the streets. I have talked to many other Portuguese who have had similar experiences. The Portuguese are very cruel to one another in France. That night, sleeping on the streets, I was so afraid that people who saw us would just say "more Portuguese," wishing that we would all go home. It is so hard to maintain one's self-respect here.

It was already summer by then and luckily we found work for a month taking care of the house of a French family that was leaving on vacation. When the family returned, the lady offered me full-time work and I accepted it. She paid me fifteen hundred francs (three hundred dollars) a month and we had our lodgings free. My husband had a good job at a factory in Argenteuil and we were both doing quite well. But the *patroa* was very demanding and had me doing all kinds of little extras, like sewing for her. I was on the run all the time. Sometimes I began at seven in the morning and only finished at midnight. I was a maid—more than a maid.

I soon discovered that she liked to drink. Sometimes I would arrive in the kitchen in the morning and find empty bottles on the floor. The situation became more and more unbearable and finally in August of 1971 my husband and I decided to return to Portugal for good.

Fifteen days after our arrival in Portugal, I received a letter from my *patroa* offering us twenty-five hundred francs (five hundred dollars) a month. She wanted my husband to do some work in the garden and would pay him too. But I did not want to go back. I had a job in a clothing factory in Portugal and was earning the equivalent of seven francs ($1.40) a day. My husband found a job that paid about sixteen francs a day. It was difficult to readjust to such small salaries and finally my husband laughed and said he could no longer stand it. He wanted to return to France. We left in February of 1972 and I rejoined him in March. All the money we had saved during the first two years was already spent and we had to begin all over again.

My husband first took a job as a plumber, and later as a solderer — his preferred profession. We rented a house abandoned by another Portuguese man who was returning to Portugal and I eventually found cleaning work. Only later did I find my present work in the clinic. I began by working at the clinic for part of the day, and then doing cleaning in private houses for the rest of the day. But it made me very tired, so now I only work in the clinic. The work there is underpaid, but it is better than working for a *patroa* who is always finding extra things for you to do. At the clinic you have specific tasks each day, no more, no less. I work in shifts — one week in the morning, the other week in the afternoons. When I work the morning shift my husband and I hardly see one another because he works from three to eleven in the evening every day. When I am home alone I do my housework. I learned how to embroider and crochet when I was a girl, so I make things for myself and for my daughters in the time I have to myself.

My morning shift begins at half-past seven. At a quarter to eight we serve breakfast. While the women are eating (it is a maternity clinic) we wash the bathrooms. I work with one other woman. When breakfast is over, she cleans the rooms and I wash the dishes. I join her when I am done with the dishes, but a half-past eleven we have to stop to prepare lunch, even if we have not finished our cleaning chores. We begin to wash the lunch dishes, but if we do not finish by half-past one, the second shift takes over. The chores are similar during the afternoon, but I prefer the morning shift because then you can go home knowing that the work for the day is done.

The boss could not be better. She does not stand over our shoulders watching everything we do. If things are not finished one day, we can leave them until the next. Besides, we know better than she does what has to be done. We are paid each month, but if we miss a day of work we lose our pay. We do, however, have a pension and paid vacations. I like the work at the clinic though I would prefer to have a factory job. In a factory you have a skill that you can take a certain pride in. I work for the money but I think that even if I were rich I might continue to work if I had a good job in a clothing factory. I would pay someone to clean my house and continue to work because I find the work satisfying. Besides, it is important for a woman to work, to help her husband. A car does not operate with two wheels. You need four!

The French women we work for here do very little, however—a bit of shopping, that is all. They spend their time smoking cigarettes and going out to cafes. They have so much time on their hands and so much freedom that they begin to look at other men. If a woman works, she does not have time for this. The poorer a couple is, the more they stay together. They do not want to bring any further problems upon themselves.

Sometimes we even see the French men doing more of the household chores than their wives. For the Portuguese it is different. There are Portuguese women here who have four children to care for and also work cleaning for others. They get little help from their husbands because in Portugal it is not the custom for men to do housework. Sometimes they will put something on the stove, take the laundry in if it is raining, or take the children out, but rarely do they wash clothes or do the dishes. They go out in the evenings and leave the work for their wives. But it is woman's work anyway. My husband might do some housework if I were sick and we were alone, but if some outsider, even my mother, were there, we would not do it. He would feel embarrassed. In France, my husband helps out more because French men do, but not in Portugal. If he did things around the house in Portugal he would only make the other men angry.

Marriage is a partnership, something to be worked out. Many women are afraid to assert themselves. The more afraid you are, the worse it is. Men are soft inside. If you assert yourself, he won't hit you. Just leave the house and come back later when things are calmer; that is the solution. The marriage vows are the same for both, but many women are not aware of their rights. Even if men have more freedom when they are single, they should be faithful after they are married. If a man complains about his wife, that she always serves him potatoes and only potatoes and that some other woman serves rice, he should realize that if he goes to the other woman he may only get rice.

My husband entrusts me with all his money. I buy everything for the house. When we want to purchase something important, however, I always discuss it with him. But sometimes, even if he does not agree, I go and buy it anyway. My husband is never angry about things like that; only about times when I talk to another man or want to wear pants. It is over a woman's behavior that a man has real control. For that we have a saying in Portugal, *Em casa manda ela, mas nela mando eu* ("In the home she rules, but I rule her"). If a man really loves his wife, he will be jealous. He is jealous because he does not think that women can control themselves. He knows that other men try to tempt women, just as he does.

I would never have another man in the house if my husband was not here. Anyone would try to take advantage of such a situation, even men who are friends of my husband's. I do not know why some men go after married women, perhaps to cuckhold (*fazer cornos*) another man. I remember a man in Portugal who always used to wait outside the factory where I worked. Once I told him that I was married, and to leave me alone. He did not believe me so I proved it to him with my identity card. He told me that my husband should be proud of me because there were not many serious women like me around. "Answer always as you have answered today," he told me.

We have a few friends here with whom we visit, mostly other married couples. It is different from Portugal where a man has his friends and a woman hers. My husband used to go out to the taverns and I stayed at home. I had girlfriends from work before I was married, but when we all married, we drifted apart. It is too expensive to have friends in Portugal; you always feel obligated to put on a show for them, but you never have the money. With family it is different. In France, we have money to entertain friends, but we want to save too, so when we visit with people, it is only a few times a month and on the weekends.

Our closest friends are a couple who live in Argenteuil. The man is the brother of the man who first helped my husband to emigrate. We see each other two or three times a month. They are friends to talk to and to share confidences with. They are not married and each of them has a spouse in Portugal; she followed him here because her husband was not good to her. They have been in France together for five years and want to remain because of all the personal difficulties that would face them in going back.

The only other couple we see frequently live near by. The man works with my husband. It took me quite a while to get to know his wife, but now we are very friendly and we even see one another in

Portugal during vacations. The one couple we know who live nearby we met through the Portuguese Service Center. We became involved in their lives because my husband helped the man find work. But I do not like his wife much; she is the kind of woman who puts her tongue to work. They are always asking for things and give nothing in return. They have six children and hardly enough money to support them. We have enough problems of our own without worrying about theirs.

We are here in France to work and save, not to socialize, and it is best, in the long run, to keep to the straight and narrow. Many Portuguese immigrants are jealous of one another. Such jealousies do not exist as much in Portugal because everyone lives in poverty. But emigration creates competition. When people first came here they helped one another, but what began to happen was that those who were helped remained ungrateful and sometimes began to say bad things about their friends. People stopped helping one another. If you help someone, you are always afraid that the person will become more successful than you are and you do not like that, for someone else to come out on top. A new Portuguese immigrant fails to understand that someone else has been in France longer and that his greater success in only natural. They want to be rich right away. They come without thinking that it costs money to live here.

To be successful is what counts and sometimes people do not go back to Portugal because they are ashamed of what others there will say about their not being rich. Others go back for good without realizing that the money will soon disappear and that their life there will take on the same rhythm it had before. That is what happened to us. You spend everything to amuse yourself, to show off, and then at some point it is all gone and you have to begin all over, guarding your escudos carefully. Only in France does your life really improve. I guess we will stay here. That is what my husband wants. He wants to bring our daughters and then forget about Portugal forever. He has even talked about taking French citizenship.

It will be a big adjustment for my daughters. They do not even want to come. My eldest daughter told me this last summer that she would run away if I made her come. She has friends in Portugal, even boyfriends. But you cannot let them have their way all the time. My mother is also against their coming. She wrote to me telling me that my girls had been saying that if I had another baby then they would not have to emigrate. She encourages them to say such things because she wants to keep them with her. My mother is sick now and cannot look after them well. We are well established here and have even sent money for my mother to buy a house in Portugal. The tables are turned from the time when my parents were helping us out.

What I would like to do eventually is to have a house in Portugal that we could use as a vacation house. If we bring our daughters here they will learn to speak and live in French. Perhaps they will even marry Frenchmen. Then, what use would it be to us to go back to Portugal? My parents will die before my daughters and ourselves and there will be no one there to visit except my brothers and sister, and I am not especially close to them. But at the same time, if anything were to happen to my husband, I would go back for good because I would have no reason to stay in France.

My husband and I think differently about the education of our daughters. He wants them to go as far as possible and will spank them if they do not study hard. But I was brought up with the belt and I do not think it is a good way. I would prefer them to go at their own pace and to choose what they want to do with their lives after they have finished their obligatory education. I would prefer to find work that they could do at home, like sewing. I would not like them to work as I do. I will not be as strict with my daughters as my parents were with me. I want to raise them according to the life of today. I will let them invite friends over if they want to. That way I can supervise them.

What worries me the most is that I will have to watch my daughters carefully when they come to France. It will be hard because I will have to work. In Portugal, boys and girls go to separate schools, but in France they are mixed together. They teach them "those things"[7] in the classroom and what is to prevent them from trying? Some women at work told me that when their daughters' periods began they were going to give them the pill in order to avoid any trouble. That is terrible. I would rather warn my daughters of the consequences and then supervise them as much as I can in order to avoid the trouble. When I was in Portugal last summer, I told my daughters to come to see me if they had any questions or heard anything from older girls. I would tell them a few things to make them afraid. Usually a girl in Portugal is told nothing. I learned about it one day when I overheard an old man talking to a pregnant girl. I did not believe it, but I was too ashamed to ask my mother if it was true. I am not against birth control. I use the pill myself, although my doctor thinks that my kidney trouble may have been caused by the pill. If I have to go off it, I will try to find some other method because if not I will be pregnant for sure. My husband is not very careful. It is not only that I do not want more children, but also because my pregnancies were hard. When my first child was born, I was in the hospital for a month afterwards.

We plan to return to Portugal for the communion of my daughters during the summer (1975). It is important that the parents are there. I want to bring them up in the Catholic faith, at least until their communion, even though I no longer attend mass. I used to belong to a Protestant congregation in Porto,[7] but here there is a church only in Paris and that is far away. My husband takes no interest in church. In the city, fewer people go to church than in the country-side because no one much cares if you go or not. Many people have no time. You have to do your housework on the weekends because you work all week. But not going to church does not mean that I do not believe in God. Sometimes I just get angry with things that the Church does. I was once in Moncao in the north of Portugal. There everyone has to give things to the church as an obligation. That is silly. The priest has his own salary. Why should he ask for more? People are losing their religion because it costs too much. It used to cost money even to get married in the church and sometimes the people were so poor that they only had a civil wedding. When I was married I had to pay one hundred and fifty escudos to have my husband's name added to my own and the marriage documents cost almost five hundred escudos.

Many people in Portugal wear black in honor of the dead. The length of time varies with the relationship of the person who has died. I still wear a black skirt for my mother-in-law because I feel uneasy in bright colors. But when I go to Portugal, I wear all black and my husband puts on a black arm band. No one here knows that we have any dead, but there, the tongues move if you are not in black.

Emigration is harder for a man than for a woman. When the woman comes, the house is usually already found and the papers are arranged. Jobs are not hard to find. The only problem is one of adapting to new things. For a woman it is perhaps more shocking to see couples kissing in the streets. A man is less shocked. Perhaps he just wishes he were in the place of the other man! A man is more used to the world outside than a woman is. The work is hard, the life is hard, but we are accustomed to that. Sometimes in Portugal we work harder than the men. This is especially true of the women who work on the land. The only difference with work in France is that you have to be willing to work on Sundays. The French do not like to, so the immigrants have to. The immigrants are in France so that the French can relax.

The best thing about working in France as a cleaning lady is that it is much easier. There you are always on your knees, and treated badly, like a slave. Here if you have been in a place for some time, the *patroa* treats you like one of the family. In Portugal, the dirtier the job is, the less you are paid. In France it is different. A man in construction earns more than a postman. People are more equal here. In Portugal, even if you earn a lot of money in France, you can never be one of *os ricos*. You do not know how to speak correctly. Country people have a heavy way of walking and rich people a different way, more elegantly. It is true, as many say, that when I go back to Portugal I feel "French". I feel superior. But in France I feel inferior. I always think about the fact that I have come to eat the bread of the French. They do not really want us here. They do not like foreigners. There are some immigrants who take things from the garbage. I have seen things thrown out that I think could be useful, but I would never touch it. The French see these people rummaging through the garbage and say *C'est un portugais*. That makes me ashamed to admit that I too am Portuguese.

But I am not complaining, because our lives are so much better here. We are not poor anymore. My husband has changed enormously. Emigration has made him a man. He realizes now how much he had made others suffer in the past. He listens to and respects me more. When my parents urged me to leave him during those troubled years before France, I refused because I accepted my marriage and my problems as my destiny. You marry just one man. I am afraid to be too happy here because any time things might go badly again. Deep down I miss Portugal and the sense of being secure in my own country. I always think about my next visit there. When I went back "for good" the first time, my father whistled. My mother told me that when I was in France he never whistled. The same is true of me. I am a martyr of life. I used to sing a lot and talk to people but now I prefer just to stay at home, do my job and not talk to anyone. Perhaps this comes with age, but it is not the only reason. It is Portugal I miss and my daughters and my mother. Even after I was married and had so much trouble with my husband I still sang. But here, if I sing something bad happens so I am never at ease. I think if I went back for good it would be different. I would be gay again, and sing . . . But my husband never wants to go back there. He thinks the life is better here. Once our children come he does not even want to go there for vacations. But I do not want to cut my daughters off so abruptly from the life there. And then, there is my mother. She might come to visit but never to stay. Other women perhaps do not feel as strongly as I because they are not so close to their mothers. Sometimes I think how horrible it would be if my mother were to die while I was here. I am here because of my husband. He told me to go back to be with my mother and my children, but I want to be with him too. So I am pulled in both directions. That is the life of the immigrant.

The city of Porto from the Douro river.

AFTERWORD

Five Years Later

On numerous occasions, social scientists working on migration have made reference to the advantage of follow-up studies which would permit a clearer illustration of the dynamic aspects of migration and migrant decision making. However, few such studies have materialized because of the methodological problems entailed in following a mobile population, particularly when the number of cases is large. Since this book deals in depth with three cases and with women whom I came to know quite well, it is possible to include a "five years later" update to their stories. During the summer of 1980, I returned to Paris and, with a little effort, I was able to find both Ricardina and Ana.

Ricardina was living at the same address in the seventeenth arrondissement where she said that they would remain for as long as they lived in France. Since her sons were older, she had taken on hourly cleaning in addition to her duties as concierge. Three days a week, she travels to the Etoile (a twenty minute metro ride) to work for a French woman who recently moved from her own neighborhood. Every night, she cleans a local bank and two local office buildings. Often her husband and children accompany her and together they complete the job more rapidly. This nightly work pays twenty francs per hour (approximately five dollars). This is less than she earns in private domestic service, but the office jobs are undeclared and it is therefore twenty francs tax free.

Ricardina expressed concerns about her children similar to those she had voiced five years earlier. Her eldest son is "lazy" and may not pass the school year. "He likes to be with his friends on the streets rather than to study." Her health continues to trouble her and recently she has had a minor operation. Her mother is now extremely ill and hardly moves from her bed. "It makes me cry, but I have my own life here and can do very little to care for her."

Ricardina talked of having purchased a five-room apartment in Lisbon which she and her husband are planning to rent. Although she would like to live in Lisbon herself, her husband does not want to. Consequently, they have also bought a plot of land in Trancoso, the provincial town closest to their native villages. They intend to build a house on this property as soon as possible. When they return to Portugal for good, they will be able to live well off the income from the Lisbon apartment, the interest on their savings, and the fruits of the land that they own in their villages. Her husband will not, she said, work for someone else once he is back in Portugal.

Slowly, Ricardina and Manuel appear to be building up their nest egg. However, the five-year interim had not brought any dramatic changes overall—they remain in the stationary limbo between a long-range intention to return to Portugal one day and the short-range desire to earn more money. The job overloading is the pivot around which these short- and long-term plans revolve, and is particularly noteworthy in a couple that has been in France for over a decade. The constant postponement of the final act of departure is characteristic of a pattern of behavior that Ricardina had previously ascribed so well to her migrant compatriots—*quando mais tem, mais querem* ("the more they have, the more they want"). Curiously, however, Ricardina remains critical in others of the very things that appear to guide her own life. Furthermore, she justifies keeping open the return option by her continued belief that "the French don't want us here." She made reference, for example, to the 1976 French government's attempt to offer money as an incentive to migrants contemplating a definite return. In short, Ricardina and Manuel's migration strategy has remained unaltered, and in remaining unaltered it has prevented them from becoming better integrated into the French way of life. They continue to live very much as immigrants and as foreigners despite the fact that their sons have been raised in no other country but France.

The relative absence of change and decisiveness in Ricardina's situation can be contrasted with the transformations and resolution in Ana's life during the five years between 1975 and 1980. The family has been reunited, a decision taken, in Domingos's words, to "stop Ana from crying every night." When the girls arrived, the family moved to less expensive lodgings in Ermont, a suburb immediately west of Eaubonne. They occupy half of a long, low building that belongs to a local church. Domingos built partitions to create two bedrooms, a living area, a bathroom, and a kitchen. In front, there is a large yard where the dog they have owned since it was a puppy is able to roam freely.

Domingos continues to work for the same employer but he is now a *chef d'équipe* ("foreman"). Ana now works for an hourly wage in a factory where metal tops for perfume bottles are made. She found the job through a newspaper ad. Most of her coworkers are French, but she claims to feel at home and to enjoy the work. Both daughters appear to be completely adjusted to life in France although Ana described the tears she shed when she first took them to school four years earlier. The eldest is bright and aggressive and has already decided that she wants to work as an interpreter for an agency that runs travel tours. Domingos is eager to see his offspring go as far as they can. "A diploma is necessary, but even so, it is hard for them to find work. One must have contacts." Through a French friend he had found his eldest daughter a summer job in a Parisian bank.

Ana lamented the fact that her daughters were growing up so quickly. "I never imagined five years ago that they would be as they are today." To elaborate on her mother's statement, the eldest daughter noted that she was more "developed" than girls her own age in Portugal. "They think only about marriage and they marry young. They do not think about a good job." In a similar vein, she was critical of Portuguese parents who are "slaves to money" and who take their children out of school as soon as they reach sixteen. "They earn a lot of money and then at the end of their lives they are too old to enjoy it."

Every member of the family has taken French citizenship and they speak French together on occasion. Domingos explained that they had not abandoned their Portuguese nationality, but took French nationality as well to protect their situation as immigrants. "We still do not know if someday the French will try to get rid of all immigrants. Having French citizenship is our security against this. It will also help my daughters to find good jobs." How different this attitude is from that of Ricardina and Manuel.

Although Ana and Domingos plan to stay permanently in France now that their family has been reunited, they have bought a plot of land near Ana's mother's house and they would like to build a home of their own where they can receive friends when they are in Portugal on vacation. When I asked them why they had finally resolved to stay for good in contrast to many of their compatriots who still dream of returning someday, Ana noted that perhaps it was because they had come originally from the city. "We have always worked for others, earned salaries, and been used to the routine of factory work." Indeed, in contrast with Ricardina, Ana and her family seem to be very well assimilated to life in France. They claim that they live like the French—they go to movies and restaurants when they feel like it. Whether it is past experience or a particular perspective deriving from their urban origins, or whether it is because they decisively altered their original migration strategy by having their children join them, the Fernandes seem to be able to work within the system and in a myriad of small ways they have adopted France as their new home.

The different perspectives of these two women is perhaps best summed up in their comments about what people could learn by reading their stories. Ricardina thought that it would be good for others to read it to understand some of the suffering that she has had to endure in her life. Ana, however, took the comment further and it is worth quoting her response in full for it shows a very special perception.

> They will see all the troubles and suffering that we have had to undergo to make a life for ourselves, but what I most want people to know about us, and about other Portuguese immigrants, is that we have succeeded. Too often the films on television that are about immigrants end at the beginning. They show all the problems we have with language, finding jobs and housing, adjusting to new food and new customs. But that is where they stop, at the beginning, not at the end.

Unlike Ana and Ricardina, Virginia Caldas was no longer in France in 1980. However, I maintained a correspondence with her after leaving Paris myself and saw her in Portugal during the summer of 1978. Just before Christmas in 1977, I received the following letter from her:

Madame Carolina:

And so, how are you? Good, I hope. And your family, I hope that they are also well. I am better. Dona Carolina, I am writing you these words to give you important news. The day I have awaited for so many years has arrived and I hope that I will be happy. 20 December, my day of departure, is a day I will never forget. My son is very pleased. He is anxiously waiting for me. Every Friday he has telephoned me. His father has sent me the money for the tickets. I only await the day when the papers and the tickets are ready. I only regret that you are far away because I would like to have you there on the day I marry. But I also want to say that even if you cannot be there for my wedding, maybe you can be in Portugal next summer for the marriage of our son.

In March or April, my son's father (I hope that by that time I will already be able to say my husband) and I will go to Portugal to rest a bit. There we will await our son. I enclose the address in Venezuela, and you already know my name. This will all be a surprise for my family. They will only know about it after I have arrived in Venezuela.

On 17 December, there will be a dinner for all the Portuguese in Neuilly and they will celebrate my departure as well as that of Father Anthony who is returning to Portugal. All this I will leave with nostalgia (*saudade*), but I hope that my life ahead will not be worse. I hope that everything will come to me as I have so hoped for. My *patroa* already misses me and I her. I do not even want to think that I am going. I have been in France for six years and during that time I have made many friends. I will miss it all.

Dona Carolina, I hope that you have a merry Christmas and a New Year full of gladness in the company of your loved ones. Christmas for me this year is a dream that I will never forget.

Virginia Caldas

The events leading up to this letter and the aftermath are worth describing because they have taken Virginia to yet another country of immigration and into a new life after more than twenty years as an unwed mother.

Virginia's son, Joaquim, was unable to find a job in Portugal after he finished his military service. Although Virginia tried to find employment for him in France, this proved impossible, largely because France had closed her doors to new immigrants (even family members of those already in France) in 1976. Simultaneously, after almost four years of silence, Joaquim's father wrote to him from Venezuela. When Joaquim replied to his father that he had no job, his father sent him a plane ticket to Venezuela. (It was a round trip ticket so that, if Joaquim did not like Venezuela, he had the option of returning).

Joaquim left Portugal during the summer of 1977, setting out as a young man of twenty-four to meet his father for the first time. His father had been very successful and was an associate owner of a business—a combination restaurant, hotel, gas station, and store—in Barcelona, Venezuela. Father and son took an immediate liking to one another. Joaquim was put in charge of the accounts and everything appeared to be going well. However, the father soon noticed that his son was not totally happy. When he finally queried, his son responded that he wanted his mother close to him. The reunion of his parents was thus engineered, and five days before Christmas in 1977, Virginia flew to Venezuela from Paris to meet the man who had fathered her son more than two decades earlier and whom she had not seen for just as long. In Venezuela, Virginia and Manuel were married in a civil ceremony and in March of 1978 they returned to Portugal. Manuel saw his aged mother for the first time in over twenty years. They remained in Portugal throughout the spring and in early June, Joaquim returned to be married to his *namorado* Iria. Both couples subsequently returned to Venezuela.

During the spring of 1980, they all returned once more to Portugal. Virginia and her husband bought a *quinta* (a large house and land) in Iria's village and they remained there for a few months. Then Manuel returned to Venezuela and a few weeks later he called Virginia to join him. Reluctantly she went, leaving her son and daughter-in-law behind.

When I saw Virginia in 1978, she was no longer as exuberant as she had been in the letter of six months earlier. Marriage had changed her and she had lost some of her former spark and gaiety. It was as if her life had taken the turn that she described in the dictums she had quoted to me previously about single girls and married women and which she subconsciously foresaw in the phrase "I hope it will not be worse" included in her December letter.

Her husband, Virginia said, did not like to dance, so she could no longer dance. "I have had my time for festas." He did not even like her to talk about her life in France (as if he were embarrassed by it or jealous of the freedom and independence which she had enjoyed for more than twenty years). While she had written to me regularly between 1975 and 1978, her letters have become fewer and fewer since her marriage. Her family explains that this is because her husband does not want her to write to anyone, especially not to someone she had known in France. Her freedom to come and go has also been limited. One of her friends in the village commented that one day she had seen Virginia in the square, accompanied by her new sister-in-law. When the friend commented to her "you never had to be chaperoned before," Virginia apparently responded *como era e como sou* ("what I was and what I am").

Virginia seems to have adopted, in an about-face sort of way, all of the aspects of docility and obedience characteristic of many Portuguese women of her generation. Her years of living alone and of supporting herself were not enough to alter her understanding of the appropriate roles for men and women within marriage, roles for which her parents had served as excellent models. Of course, the changes in her behavior are also in response to a husband who clearly wishes to command. It may be that he has never forgiven her for the "original sin" that she committed in giving herself to him years earlier. Certainly, his excessive suspicion of her life in France is indicative of such feelings.

Members of her family feel that this is so and some express the view that Virginia would have been better off staying in France—that twenty-five years is a long time between a first romance and its rekindlement. There is also some feeling that Virginia remains distressed and ashamed because she has not been married in the Church. The complications stem, it seems, from the fact that Manuel had been married when he was in Brazil. This first wife left him and he was later divorced. Whether a Church wedding will ever occur, whether Virginia will ever settle happily into married life, and whether the storybook ending of a *casa portuguesa* will ever be realized remain to be seen.

One final point is worth re-emphasizing in this Afterword. While the stories of Ricardina, Ana, and Virginia were originally chosen because they represented three distinct initial patterns of emigration for Portuguese women, it is curious that, five years later, the courses that each of their lives has followed remain different. Ricardina and Ana, and, for that matter, Manuel and Domingos, have adapted in alternative ways to continued life in France. Their backgrounds, one rural, the other urban, help to explain the different methods of coping and the different ambitions and goals that they have set for themselves. Virginia has departed, as she predicted, but for a reason that was unexpected both by her and by me, and to a new life which, five years earlier, she only imagined. Clearly, migration does not involve a one-time, irreversible decision. Nor does life as a migrant necessarily develop according to the coherent plan that many individuals set out for themselves prior to their departure. Adjustments and alterations are made as new opportunities arise, as new hurdles are faced.

Conclusion

The New Portuguese letters written by the Three Marias includes an imaginary letter from a fictional peasant woman, Maria Ana, to her husband, an emigrant in Canada. Maria Ana writes:

> Even though you've spared me the many hardships and miseries that so many people around here are suffering . . . it's as though I were wearing widow's weeds because I'll be thirty-eight this year and I bore you three children before you went away and now they're all grown up and in all these years that you've been away I've never done anything to tarnish your reputation and when I shed so many tears last time you left again you gave me your word you'd send for me to join you there in that faraway place . . . but then you wrote telling me to wait till you'd set aside enough money to make your children rich. . . . I'm worn out and dying of loneliness because a woman without a man is like barren earth and a bake oven that there is no use lighting . . . I don't have any idea whether you really will come back since all you ever talk about is how hard you're working and how much money you're making.[1]

As one embodiment of the spirit of Portuguese womanhood, this Maria Ana archetype is witness to the emigration that permeates Portuguese society. The passage and statistical evidence make it clear that numerous Portuguese children have been raised without their fathers and many Portuguese wives have shared their bed with their husbands for only a small part of their married lives. The absent father became a role model for boys who grew to adulthood with the expectation that they too would emigrate. Although the destinations changed as the world economy changed, departure from the homeland was, nevertheless, part of an almost predetermined life plan. For young girls, the role model and the expectations were different. At most they migrated internally, and while still single, to become part of the population of domestic servants working for the urban and rural upper classes. However, many simply remained at home. Indeed, just as women today in developing countries are assuming responsibility for economic activities customarily performed by men, but abandoned by them as they enter into labor migration or other capital-intensive activities, peasant women in Portugal have been doing "men's work" for more than a century. This fact in itself makes it difficult to fit Portuguese peasant women neatly into models such as those developed by Ester Boserup in her book on women's roles in economic development or by anthropologists writing about the public and private domains of men and women in peasant societies throughout the world. Portuguese peasant women are not relegated to the domestic sphere as are women in other areas of settled plough agriculture. Rather, they have shared agricultural duties en par with men or, with their husbands absent, have assumed total responsibility for farming the land. However, while Portuguese peasant women, as well as Portuguese urban working-class women, conceive of their economic roles as complementary to those of their husbands, this complementarity does not necessarily imply equality. Indeed, both legal and moral codes have operated in Portugal, as in other areas of the Mediterranean, to define the social status of women and to limit their power and authority. On the one hand, these moral codes, and the ideology that dictates separate spheres of influence and activity for men and women thrives in Portugal as a result of the support given them by the bourgeois and upper classes. Yet it is also possible to suggest that the tradition of male emigration among the lower, and particularly the peasant sectors of Portuguese society has given them added cultural centrality. In the absence of fathers and husbands, the concept of shame, the social and moral value placed upon virginity and chastity, and even popular adages such as *A mulher e a ovelha, com sol a cortelha* ("Women and sheep, with the sun to the stable") are necessary to restrain the behavior of "independent" women; that is, women who do not have men around to control them. The peasant Maria Ana conceived by the Three Marias specifically mentions that she has "done nothing to tarnish [her husband's] reputation." The refutation implies, however, that the possibility exists.

Although there are still many living Maria Anas in Portugal today, the postwar phase of Portuguese emigration, and particularly emigration to France, has been distinctive in affording women a greater opportunity to become actors in the emigration process. This has required a different set of adaptations from those necessary in accustoming oneself to life as a "living widow" in the village.

The burgeoning literature that treats the subject of women as actors in migration emphasizes what Lisa Peattie has referred to as the "complexity of trade-offs amongst which women construct their lives as they move in response to market opportunities."[2] For Portuguese women in France, one such trade-off is represented in the experiences of Ana Fernandes who, for several years, gave up her role as mother in favor of her duties as wife, duties which are both economic—in the sense of being a joint breadwinner—and social-psychological—in the sense of her obligations to care for her husband and to serve as his companion. Clearly, single migrant women who have fewer role conflicts do not have to make as many complex decisions. A second trade-off involves the kinds of economic roles that migrant women assume in the place of immigration. Again, the family is pitted against the possibilities for higher earnings and a sacrifice has to be made in one realm or the other. Although not directly treated in this volume through the three stories presented, there are Portuguese women in France who do not work. Their reasons vary: they have large families and no one to help them care for the children; their husbands do not want them to work; they are themselves afraid to work, or feel that they are too old. However, it can be maintained that these women are less well adapted to life in France than those Portuguese migrant women who do have some form of employment. For these latter women, the changes brought about through migration are perhaps more significant since the complementary economic roles that they played in Portugal are undermined by a distinct separation of the home and the workplace in the urban environment. Even Ana Fernandes' pattern of migration is understandable in these terms. Raised as an urban working-class woman, she expects to be gainfully employed. However, without her mother to help her with her children, the only real alternative, as she first saw it, was to leave her children behind. By the time that her daughters did join her in France, they were old enough to require less constant supervision.

Although some of the recent literature on migrant women deals with the preservation of traditional relationships of male dominance-female subordination among unemployed migrant women (Denich 1976, McLaughlin, 1975), most studies focus on changes in the status of women resulting from new forms of productive economic activity in the place of immigration or in-migration. For example, Bloch (1976), in a paper on Polish immigrant women in the United States, notes their emerging independence as a consequence of their increasingly important economic contributions to the support of the Polish immigrant family. Foner (1975) discusses the superior wage-earning opportunities for Jamaican women in England, a factor that "buttresses their claims to power and respect in relations with their husbands and gives them a greater independence in England than in Jamaica."[3]

The Portuguese women who have told their stories in the present volume do mention some of these aspects of change, but it is not clear that it is their economic roles per se that have given them a greater sense of freedom and independence. Indeed, they all played similar roles in Portugal and were relatively self-sufficient there prior to their emigration. Wage earning is for them an obligation, not an advantage. This can be seen in the desires of Ricardina, Virginia, and many other migrant women of rural backgrounds to become *donas da casa* ("homemakers"). This position represents for them an improvement in status, particularly with the examples provided by their employers in France or their former employers in Portugal.

What all three women do emphasize as a major change is the sense of freedom that emigration has given them from the *vida escrava* of the Portuguese lower class woman. While this conception of a "slave's life" is based in part on the heavy economic burdens that often fall to women in Portugal, it is also a result of the legal, social, and cultural definitions of the status of women in pre-1974 Salazarist Portugal and the restrictions that all of these definitions imposed upon the behavior of women. The choice of the word "slave" has, therefore, significance on several levels—slave to the legally and culturally defined male master, and slave within Salazarist Portugal's highly hierarchized society. Thus, while migration within Portugal might have given a young peasant girl a certain degree of economic independence, it was not liberating in the same way as migration to France because it did not afford the opportunity to live according to a different set of social and cultural codes or legal rights. The importance of the "liberating" or "freeing" aspects of emigration to France are evident in what Ricardina and Virginia present as the major motive for their respective departures. Certainly a desire to improve their lives in an economic sense was a factor, but the wish to escape social oppression or embarrassment was clearly the stronger motivating force. For married women, the different social codes extend to domestic roles that make the sharing of household duties and leisure time between men and women acceptable in France. It is perfectly understandable that what Portuguese men are willing to do in France, they are not so willing to do in Portugal. The social expectations for behavior are simply different. One other young woman interviewed put it quite succinctly:

> My husband likes to go out with his friends in Portugal. He reverts to his old ways. For me it will be hard if we ever go back for good for this reason. I like us to do things together and I have told my husband that I will insist on it if we return. In Portugal, women have never insisted. They remain quiet. In France, it is better.

Not only is it better because the status of women is defined differently in France than it was in Salazarist Portugal, but also because of the greater interdependence of a migrant husband and wife, each of whom are uprooted from the traditional milieu where male and female spheres are more distinct and where a network of familial or communal associations provide an alternative to the company of each other.

The relationship between a woman's status in her own society and migration is one that has been examined in many other parts of the world. According to Kudat (1975) and Kiray (1976), Turkish women see migration as a means by which to "free themselves from inferior status in their household," a status that defines them essentially as outsiders in a house full of their husband's kinsmen. Migration means the formation of an independent nuclear family. Rogers (1976) describes a similar motivation among French peasant women of the Auvergne region who migrate to escape a life as daughter-in-law within their husband's stem family. The migration of Irish peasant women is a further example. In a system where a single male heir is selected to remain on the farm and the fate of all other siblings, both male and female, is to remain celibate or to emigrate, a woman—whether as a celibate "spinster" in her brother's household or as a wife with no property—is in a much more subordinate social position than a woman who has a clear right to a portion of the family patrimony. The latter is more characteristic of rural Portugal, particularly northern Portugal, a fact that is probably an explanation for the different historical patterns of emigration and celibacy in Portugal and Ireland.

However, in the postwar period, and with emigration to France, opportunities for female emigration have increased, and the latent push factors associated with the way of life distinctive to women have played a more important role in their decisions to emigrate. Migration to France has provided Portuguese women with an alternative to the agricultural way of life that Portuguese men have been escaping for decades. Eventually, this will have important implications for life in the Portuguese countryside. As women of the generation of Ricardina's and Virginia's mothers pass away, there will be fewer and fewer younger women willing to continue farming the small plots of land throughout northern Portugal. This will be, perhaps, the most significant impetus for change in the regional system of agriculture in northern Portugal, a system based on tradition and still relatively impervious to modernization. The experiences of migrant women in France have expanded their sense of their rights and, although they may not be politically active in the newly revived, Lisbon-oriented, Portuguese feminist movement, their eager embracing of legal changes brought about by the new Portuguese constitution may have a major impact upon the status of women within Portuguese rural and urban working-class society and within the Portuguese family.

Appendices

Key for Genealogies

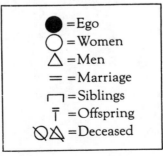

● = Ego
○ = Women
△ = Men
= = Marriage
⊓ = Siblings
⊤ = Offspring
⌀⩜ = Deceased

APPENDIX A:1
Genealogy of Ricardina dos Santos

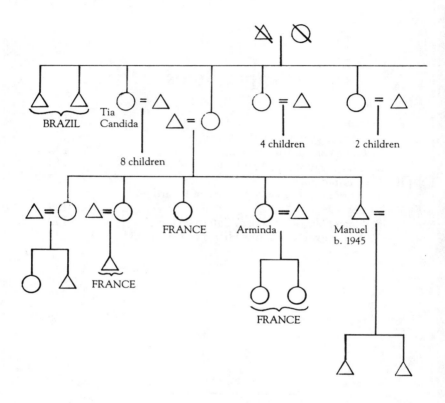

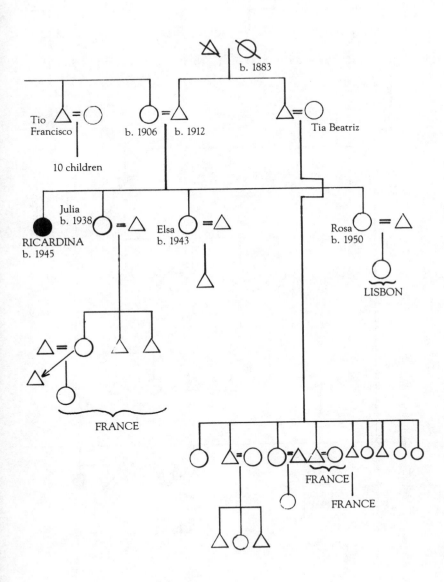

APPENDIX A:2
Genealogy of Virginia Caldas

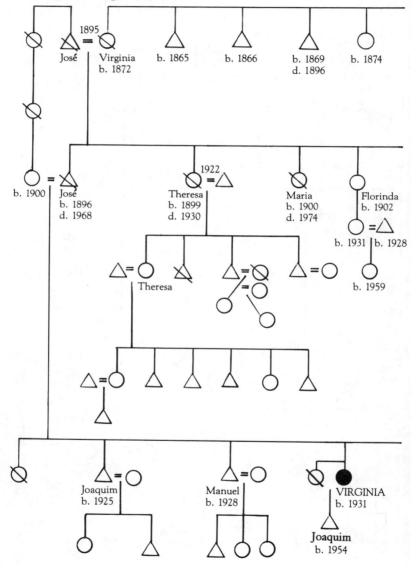

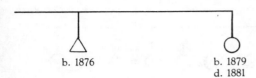

b. 1876   b. 1879
                          d. 1881

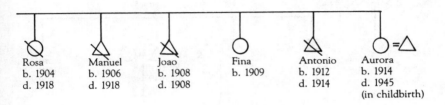

Rosa   Manuel   Joao   Fina   Antonio   Aurora
b. 1904   b. 1906   b. 1908   b. 1909   b. 1912   b. 1914
d. 1918   d. 1918   d. 1908   d. 1914   d. 1945
                                                            (in childbirth)

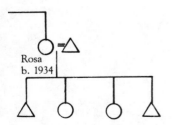

Rosa
b. 1934

APPENDIX A:3
Genealogy of Ana Fernandes

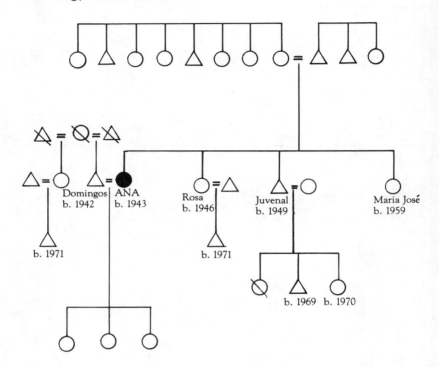

APPENDIX B:1
Work and Residence History of Ricardina dos Santos

Year	Work	Residence
1967	Hours of Cleaning (9–10/day)	a) room—alone b) maids room with nephews and niece, paid in 2 hrs. work
April 1978	Married, a few hours cleaning	Paris, hotel meublee, 250F/Mo
October 1978	A few hours cleaning	Sevres, room of employer, paid in 2 hrs. work
December 1978	returned briefly to Portugal	
1969 (first half)	without work	Paris, various hotels meublees
1969–1971	a) factory—cleaning b) cafe—cleaning 7am–4pm 800F/Mo c) hours of cleaning 7am–2pm or 1pm–8pm 600F/Mo	a) Meudon, room, 300F/Mo b) Meudon, apartment for a year, 650F/Mo, 2 lodgers
1971	without work	Paris XXeme, studio, 500F/Mo
January 1972	concierge and a few hours of cleaning	Paris XVIIeme

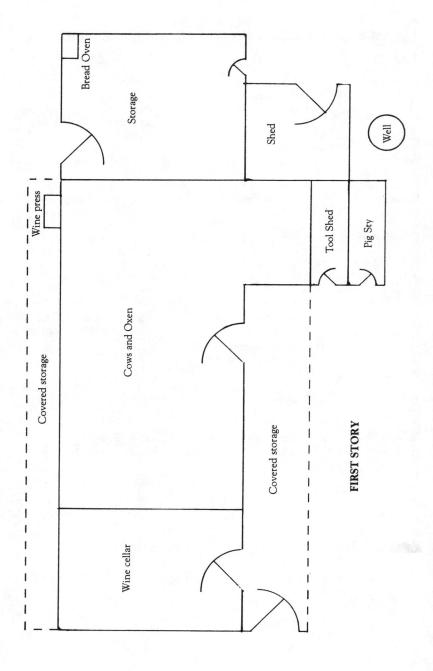

FIRST STORY

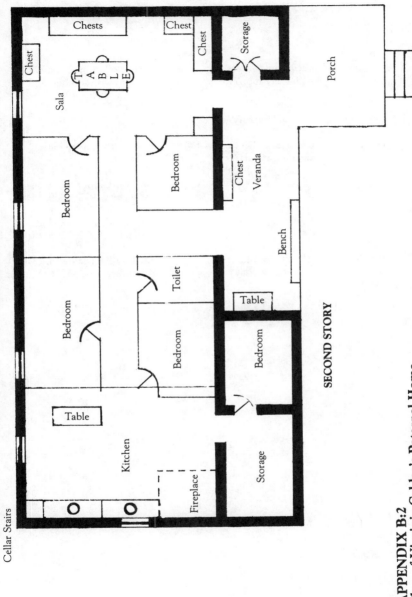

Cellar Stairs

Chests

Chest

Chest

Chest

Storage

Porch

Sala

T A
B
L
E

Bedroom

Bedroom

Chest

Veranda

Bedroom

Bedroom

Toilet

Bench

Table

Table

Bedroom

Bedroom

Kitchen

Storage

Fireplace

SECOND STORY

APPENDIX B:2
Plan of Virginia Caldas's Paternal Home

APPENDIX B:3
Work and Residence History of Ana Fernandes

Year	Work	Residence
1970	Cleaning, Monday —Sunday mornings	a) attic of a house, 150F/Mo b) room with kitchen and bath, 250F/Mo
Summer 1971	Portugal, factory work	Portugal
Spring 1972	Clinic and 3–4 hours cleaning per day	room with private bath 150F/Mo
1973	Clinic	pavillon-Eaubonne, since December, 1972, 500F/Mo
1974	Clinic	pavillon-Eaubonne, since December, 1972, 500F/Mo
October 1974	Clinic and 3 hours cleaning per day	pavillon-Eaubonne, since December, 1972, 500F/Mo

Notes

Introduction

1. I have developed this discussion in an article entitled "Is the Ethnic Community Inevitable? A Comparison of the Settlement Patterns of Portuguese Immigrants in Toronto and Paris," which has been published in *Journal of Ethnic Studies* vol. 9, no. 3 (1981): 1–17. Essentially, the article argues that due to the nature of migrant female employment (as maids, concierges) where housing is often provided to them, to the physical structure of the city of Paris (vertical rather than horizontally stratified), and to an immigration policy that has encouraged the assimilation of newcomers, ethnic communities have less of a chance of establishing themselves in a city like Paris than in a city like Toronto.

2. Much of this discussion has been systematically reviewed in Langness (1965).

3. Paul Radin, *Crashing Thunder*, pp. 46–7. See also Dollard (1935).

4. See Goodenough (1963) for the full discussion.

5. A lengthier and largely unanalyzed version of Ricardina's story was published in Portugal by the Universidade Nova de Lisboa in 1978, under the title *Já chorei muitas lágrimas: crônica duma mulher portuguesa imigrada.* See also Carolina de Jesus, *Child of the Dark: The Diary of Carolina Maria de Jesus* (New York: E.P. Dutton, 1962); and Heluiz Washburne, *Land of the Good Shadows: The Life Story of Anauta, an Eskimo Woman* (New York: Doubleday, 1940).

6. The best discussions are to be found in Barnes (1979) and Hicks (1977).

7. J.A. Barnes, *Who Should Know What?*, p. 142.

Chapter One

1. Ferreira de Castro, *Emigrantes*, pp. 32–33.

2. Charles R. Boxer, *Four Centuries of Portuguese Expansion, 1415–1825*, p. 18.

3. See Boxer (1975), Bender (1978), and Pescatello (1976) for further discussion of the importance of miscegenation in the Portuguese colonial world.

4. Joel Serrão, *Emigração portuguesa*, p. 34.

5. Portuguese census data at the close of the nineteenth century clearly shows the disproportionate sex ratio resulting from this male-dominated pattern of migration. Further discussion can be found in Livi Bacci (1971).

6. William H. Koebel, *Portugal: Its Land and People*, p. 230.

7. Aubrey Bell, *Portugal of the Portuguese*, p. 78.

8. The bibliography of this post-World War II population flow is indeed extensive. The literature varies from broad works on population problems from a pan-European perspective to those dealing with emigration from a particular country or to a particular country. The bibliography in the present volume includes references to some of these works.

9. The exact advantages of this emigration to the sending societies is an extremely controversial issue which has been raised by several authors including Rhoades (1979), Bohning (1975), and Griffin (1976).

10. Colette Callier (1966) provides a very thorough description of a female-dominated village in the upper Minho region of northern Portugal.

11. This is not to claim that there are no female immigrants in other northern European countries. While France began to support familial immigration and the regroupment of the immigrant family abroad, countries such as Germany and Switzerland have encouraged contract labor migration of both men and women and have emphasized more consistently the return of the "guest worker" to his or her homeland once the labor contract has expired. Or course, all immigration policies have been reevaluated since 1974.

12. Juliette Minces, *Les Travaillures étrangers en France*, p. 33.

13. Elina Guimarães, "Sete décadas de feminismo," p. 15.

14. Helen Lane, Preface to Maria Isabel Barreno, Maria Teresa Horta, and Maria Velho da Costa, *The Three Marias*. Lane describes the genesis of the book in private meetings and exchanges of writings between the three Marias.

15. Vaz de Carvalho, quoted in Cesar de Frias, *A Mulher*, pp. 26–27.

16. *Grande encyclopaedia portuguesa e brasileira*, 18:108, my emphasis.

17. For a discussion of the image of "the lady" see Lamphere (1975).

18. V. Vernier Contrepied, *Charme et sagesse du Portugal*, p. 176.

19. Peter Fryer and Patricia McGowan, *Le Portugal de Salazar*, p. 56.

20. João Pereira Neto, "A Familia e a sociedade portuguesa perante a industrialização," p. 10.

21. Simone de Beauvoir, *The Second Sex*, p. 113.

Chapter Two

1. I owe this information to Dr. Joachim Lopes Correia de Mora.

2. It is highly likely that this sister is no longer in Africa. The story was collected before the decolonization process began in the former Portuguese overseas territories of Angola and Mozambique.

3. Julio Dinis, *As Pupilas do senhor Reitor*, p. 236.

4. The aspiration that Portuguese women nurture to become senhoras has been described in Chapter One and is similar to that which Harkness (1973) describes among rural migrant women in Bogota, Colombia. Traditional ideas of the woman as "sheltered and revered household goddess" are maintained during migration, but "a certain level of affluence is required before these ideals can be fulfilled."

5. Antonio de Figueiredo, *Portugal and its Empire*, p. 17.

6. In the early pages of Vitor de Moigenie's turn-of-the-century volume, *A Mulher em Portugal*, the topic of courtship arises. Moigenie records a conversation with a certain Dona Candida who claims "Our greatest defect is still *o namoro*. . . . Courtship is still a frivolous vice; people court for pride, for a past-time, and for habit. . . . A woman gets used to having a *namoro* like she has an expensive dress, a book, a piano, a garden" (p. 15).

7. Jaime Cortesão, *O que o povo canta em Portugal*, p. 161.

8. Ibid., p. 130.

9. Peter Fryer and Patricia McGowan, *Le Portugal de Salazar*, p. 51.

10. de Figueiredo, op. cit., p. 26.

11. For an elaboration of this migration ideology, see Caroline B. Brettell, "Emigrar para Voltar: "A Portuguese Ideology of Return Migration" in *Papers in Anthropology* 20:1–20.

12. Ricardina used the Portuguese word *criado*, which translates as "man-servant." She is referring to young men who do farm labor on a regular basis for a particular family.

13. The couple had been married civilly, but papers were not in order for a church wedding. In the view of these rural Catholics, a marriage is not a marriage without a church ceremony.

14. The use of diminutives is extremely important in Portugal, as are titles and forms of address in general (Cintra 1972). Forms of address involve a curious mixture of proximity and distance. A Portuguese maid, for example, addresses her employer as "Senhora Dona Maria" rather than simply as "Senhora Rodrigues." The former is considered much more respectful. In a slightly different vein, but of relevance to the present discussion because of its reference to the status of women in Portugal, is an Associated Press article that appeared in the 4 November 1978 edition of the *Austin American Statesman* (p. A7):

> It was a scene that would gladden the heart of any feminist. The boss was a woman, her assistant was a woman, and the only man in sight among thirty office workers was a typist. The boss, Ana Vicente, of the Prime Minister's Commission on the Status of Women, approached the solitary male. "You may have to do these letters over again, Melo," she said. "Whatever you say, Mrs. Ana," typist Melo replied. That simple exchange illustrated just one small way in which the legalistic structure of women's equality in Portugal, painstakingly built by activists since the 1974 revolution here, falters in the face of ordinary human habit. Except for close friends who are on a first name basis, there is no form of polite conversation in Portuguese that permits men and women to address each other on equal terms. The exchange echoing centuries of male domination but spoken in an office dedicated to sexual equality left both sides uneasy. Despite equal rights, machismo lives on in Portugal—in ways that amuse or hurt and that often are scarcely noticed by the tradition-bound majority in both sexes.

Chapter Three

1. Colette Callier-Boisvert, in a manuscript entitled "Emigration et famille," notes the expression of this ideal in a song made popular by the Portuguese fadista Amalia Rodriguese entitled "Casa portuguesa":

> Four whitewashed walls
> The light perfume of rosemary
> A bunch of golden grapes
> Two rosebushes in the garden
> An image of St. Joseph in title
> And a springtime sun
> A promise of kisses
> Two arms which await me
> A Portuguese house for certain
> For certain a Portuguese house.

2. The association between emigration and celibacy becomes stronger if a country such as Ireland is considered. In rural Ireland, women do not inherit a property equally with men as they do customarily in most regions of northern Portugal. In Ireland, men also do the major farm work. Rural Ireland is characterized by high rates of male celibacy and significant female emigration. For further discussion of Ireland see Kennedy (1973) and Sheper-Hughes (1979, 1979a).

3. The frequency of illegitimacy throughout western Europe in the latter half of the nineteenth century has been treated by Shorter (1971).

4. Massimo Livi Bacci, *A Century of Portuguese Fertility*, p. 73.

5. *Promessas* are the vows that religious Portuguese Catholics make to particular saints when they want that saint to watch over them or to help them through some crisis. In the past, most *promessas* were filled by making pilgrimages to the chapel of the saint, perhaps even on one's knees. Today, they are more often fulfilled through some kind of monetary payment. For a more complete discussion of *promessas* in association with emigration see Caroline B. Brettell, "Emigrar para Voltar: A Portuguese Ideology of Return Migration" in *Papers in Anthropology* 20:1–20.

6. Virginia is referring here to a hysterectomy she had in France in the fall of 1974.

7. Elina Guimarães has provided me with further examples of similar adages in a personal communication:

Mãe o que é casar? Filha, é penar, parir, chorar
Mother, what is marriage? Daughter, it is trouble, giving birth and tears.

Quando eu era solteirinha, usava fitas aos milhos
Agora sou casada, trago lágrimas nos olhos
When I was single, I used ribbons and ties
Now that I am married, I have tears in my eyes.

Chapter Four

1. Julio Dinis, *Uma Familia inglesa*, pp. 41–42.

2. The two major forms of public housing available to immigrants in France are HLMs (Habitation à loyer modérée) and Cite de transit (transit centers). The latter were viewed primarily as places of adjustment, a stage in the move to a modern apartment building and lodged, for the most part, immigrants from North Africa and Algeria. For further discussion, see Castles and Kosack (1973).

3. A rather damning portrait of the poverty of Porto is contained in Edgar Rodrigues and Roberto das Neves, *A Fome em Portugal*. Their empathy extends particularly to the women of the urban working class who "in the fight for life . . . grovel at the feet of the senhores as in primitive times, without any regard for their physical and moral integrity . . . Whoever visits the city of Porto will see in places where garbage is thrown women and children rifling through it to find paper, old shoes, tin cans, a piece of coal" (p. 64).

4. The *cadernos* published by the Commissão da Condição Feminina in 1976 provide details and statistics on the employment of women in Portugal. See particularly numbers four through six.

5. See, for example, Friedl et al. (1967), Chinas (1973), and Wolf (1969).

6. Rio Tinto is a working-class suburb of the city of Porto.

7. She is referring here to a sex education course that was introduced into the French school system in the fall of 1974. School officials went to great lengths in some areas to explain these courses to Portuguese parents.

8. Ana was born a Catholic, but professed this interest in Protestantism. In general, the Protestants in Portugal are in the southern half of the country. She offered no further explanation of her Protestant bent.

Conclusion

1. Maria Isabel Barreno, Maria Teresa Horta, and Maria Velho da Costa, *The Three Marias*, pp. 116–119 passim.

2. Lisa Peattie, "Introduction to Migrants and Women who Wait," p. 121.

3. Nancy Foner, "Women, Work and Migration," p. 229.

Bibliography

Barnes, J.A.
  1979 *Who Should Know What? Social Science, Privacy and Ethics.* Cambridge: Cambridge University Press.

Barreno, Maria Isabel, Maria Teresa Horta, and Maria Velho da Costa
  1974 *The Three Marias: New Portuguese Letters.* Translated by Helen Lane. New York: Doubleday and Company, Inc., Bantam Books.

Bell, Aubrey
  1915 *Portugal of the Portuguese.* London: Isaac Pitman and Sons, Ltd.

Bender, Gerald
  1978 *Angola under the Portuguese: The Myth and the Reality.* Berkeley: University of California Press.

Bennett, John W. and Kurt H. Wolff
  1955 Toward communication between sociology and anthropology. In *Yearbook of Anthropology,* edited by William Thomas, pp. 329–351. New York: Wenner Gren Foundation for Anthropological Research.

Bloch, Harriet
  1976 Changing Domestic Roles among Polish Women. *Anthropological Quarterly* 49:3–10.

Bohning, W. R.
  1975 Some Thoughts on Emigration from the Mediterranean Basin. *International Labor Review* 3:251–277.

Boserup, Ester
  1970 *Women's Roles in Economic Development.* London: George Allen and Unwin.

Bossen, Laurel
1975   Women in Modernizing Societies. *American Ethnologist* 2: 587–601.

Boxer, Charles R.
1965   *Four Centuries of Portuguese Expansion, 1415–1825.* Johannesburg: Witwatersand University Press.

1975   *Mary and Misogyny: Women in Iberian Overseas Expansion, 1415–1815.* London: Duckworth.

Brettell, Caroline B.
1978a   Hope and Nostalgia: The Migration of Portuguese Women to Paris. Dissertation, Brown University.

1978b   Vamos Celebrar: Emigration and the Religious Festa in Northern Portugal. Paper presented to the 77th Annual Meeting of the American Anthropological Association, Los Angeles, November 14–18.

1979   Emigrar para Voltar: A Portuguese Ideology of Return Migration. *Papers in Anthropology*, 20:1–20.

Buechler, Judith Maria
1976   Something Funny Happened on the Way to the Agora: A Comparison of Bolivian and Spanish Galician Female Migrants. *Anthropological Quarterly* 49:62–68.

Callier, Collette
1966   Soajo, une communauté feminine rurale de l'Alto Minho. *Bulletin des études portugaises.* Lisbon-Paris, 27:237–78.

Callier-Boisvert, Colette
nd   Emigration et famille: Les *franceses* à Poitiers. Ms.

Castles, Stephen and G. Kosack
1973   *Immigrant Workers and the Class Structure in Western Europe.* London: Oxford University Press.

Castro, Armando
1972   *Estudos de historia socio-económico de Portugal.* trs. Collecâo Civilização Portuguesa. Porto: Editora Inova.

Cesar, Guilhermino
1969   O brasileiro na ficção portuguesa. Lisbon: Parceria, A.M. Pereira, Ltd.

Chinas, Beverly
1973   The Isthmus Zapotecs Women's Roles in Cultural Context. New York: Holt, Rinehart, and Winston.

Cintra, Luis F.L.
1972   Sobre formas de tratamento na lingua portuguesa. Lisbon: Livros Horizonte, Colleção Horizonte #18.

Cohen, Abner
1967   Custom and Politics in Urban Africa. Berkeley: University of California Press.

Cortesão, Jaime
1942   O que o povo canta em Portugal. Rio de Janeiro: Livros de Portugal.

Crawford, Oswald
1909   Portugal Old and New. London: Kegan Paul, Trench and Co.

Cronin, Constance
1971   The Sting of Change: Sicilians in Sicily and Australia. Chicago: University of Chicago Press.

1977   Illusion and Reality in Sicily. In Sexual Stratification: A Cross-Cultural View, edited by Alice Schlegal, pp. 67–93. New York: Columbia University Press.

Cutileiro, Jose
1971   A Portuguese Rural Society. Oxford: Oxford University Press.

de Beauvoir, Simone
1961   The Second Sex. New York: Bantam Books.

de Figueiredo, Antonio
1961   Portugal and its Empire: The Truth. London: Victor Gollancz.

1975   Portugal: Fifty Years of Dictatorship. London: Penguin.

de Frias, Cesar
nd   A Mulher. Biblioteca das Noivas. Lisbon: Aillaud et Bertrand.

de Moigenie, Vitor
   1924   *A Mulher em Portugal.* 3rd ed. Lisbon: Livraria Educação
          Nacional.

Denich, Bette
   1976   Urbanization and Women's Roles in Yugoslavia. *Anthropological
          Quarterly* 49:11–19.

Descamps, Paul
   1935   *Le Portugal: La vie sociale actuelle.* Paris: Firmin, Didot et Cie.

Dias, Jorge
   1948   *Vilarinho da furna.* Porto: Instituto para a Alta Cultura.

   1953   *Rio de onor: Comunitarismo agro-pastoril.* Porto: Instituto para a
          Alta Cultura.

   1955   Algumas considerações acerca da estrutura social do povo portu-
          gues. *Revista de Antropologia* 3:1–19.

Dinis, Julio
   1962   *Uma familia inglesa: Cenas da vida do Porto.* Porto: Livraria
          Civilização.

   1963   *As pupilas do senhor Reitor.* Porto: Livraria Civilização.

Dollard, John
   1935   *Criteria for the Life History.* New Haven: Yale University Press.

Douglass, William
   1976   Serving Girls and Sheepherders: Emigration and Continuity in a
          Spanish Basque Village. In *The Changing Faces of Rural Spain*,
          edited by Joseph Aceves and William Douglass, pp. 45–62. Cam-
          bridge: Schenkman.

Dyk, Walter
   1938   *Son of Old Man Hat: A Navaho Autobiography.* New York: Har-
          court Brace.

Ferreira de Castro
   1928   *Emigrantes.* 4th ed. Lisbon: Guimarães Editores.

Foner, Nancy
   1975   Women, Work, and Migration: Jamaicans in London. *Urban
          Anthropology* 4:229–49.

Ford, Clellan S.
1941 *Smoke from their Fires*. New Haven: Yale University Press.

Freeman, Gary P.
1979 *Immigrant Labor and Racial Conflict in Industrial Societies: The French and British Experience, 1945–1975*. Princeton: Princeton University Press.

Friedl, Ernestine, et al.
1967 Appearance and Reality: Status and Roles of Women in Mediterranean Societies. *Anthropological Quarterly* (Special issue) 40: 95–183.

Fryer, Peter and Patricia McGowan
1963 *Le Portugal de Salazar*. Paris: Editions Ruedo Ibérico.

Goodenough, Ward
1963 *Cooperation in Change: An Anthropological Approach to Community Development*. New York: Russell Sage.

Granier, R. and J.P. Marciano
1975 The Earnings of Immigrant Workers in France. *International Labor Review* 3:143–65.

Griffen, K.
1976 On the Emigration of the Peasantry. *World Development* 4:353–61.

Guimarães, Elina
1975 *Coisas de mulheres*. Porto: Editorial Promoção.

1978 Sete décadas de feminismo. Comissão da Condição Feminina Boletim 1, pp. 7–15.

Harkness, Shirley
1973 The Pursuit of an Ideal: Migration, Social Class, and Women's Roles in Bogota, Colombia. In *Female and Male in Latin America*, edited by Ann Pescatello. pp. 231–54. Pittsburgh: University of Pittsburgh Press.

Hicks, George L.
1977 Informant Anonymity and Scientific Accuracy: The Problem of Pseudonyms. *Human Organization* 36:214–20.

Kelley, Jane Holden
 1978 *Yaqui Women: Contemporary Life Histories*. Lincoln: University of
       Nebraska Press.

Kennedy, Robert E., Jr.
 1973 *The Irish: Emigration, Marriage, and Fertility.* Berkeley: University
       of California Press.

Kiray, M.
 1976 The Family of the Immigrant Worker. In *Turkish Workers in
       Europe*, edited by Nermin Abadan-Unat, pp. 210–34. Leiden: E.J.
       Brill.

Koebel, William
 1909 *Portugal: Its Land and People*. London: A. Constable and Co.,
       Ltd.

Kudat, Ayse
 1975 Structural Change in the Migrant Turkish Family. In *Manpower
       Mobility Across Cultural Boundaries*, edited by R.E. Krane, pp.
       77–94. Leiden: E.J. Brill.

Lama, Maria
 1948 *As Mulheres do meu pais*. Lisbon: Editora Actualis.

Lamphere, Louise
 1975 The Roots of Cultural Diversity Among American Women.
       Unpublished paper.

Langness, L.L.
 1965 *The Life History in Anthropological Science*. New York: Holt, Rine-
       hart, and Winston.

Lewis, Oscar
 1961 *The Children of Sánchez: Autobiography of a Mexican Family*. New
       York: Random House.

 1965 *La Vida*. New York: Random House.

Lima dos Santos, Maria de Lourdes
 1970 Contribução para uma analise sociográfica da familia em
       Portugal. *Analise Social* 29:41ff.

Levi Bacci, Massimo
 1971 *A Century of Portuguese Fertility*. Princeton: Princeton University
       Press.

Martins, Herminio
   1971   Portugal. In *Contemporary Europe: Class, Status and Powers*, edited by Margaret Scotford Archer and Salvador Giner, pp. 72–89. London: Wiedenfeld and Nicolson.

McBride, Theresa M.
   1977   The Long Road Home: Women's Work and Industrialization. In *Becoming Visible: Women in European History*, edited by Renate Bridenthal and Claudia Koonz, pp. 280-95. Boston: Houghton Mifflin Company.

Michaelson, E. and Walter Goldschmidt
   1971   Female Roles and Male Dominance among Peasants, *Southwestern Journal of Anthropology* 27:330–52.

Michel, Andree
   1974   *The Modernization of North African Families in Paris.* The Hague: Mouton.

Minces, Juliette
   1973   *Les Travailleurs étrangers en France.* Paris: Seuil.

Paine, Suzanne
   1974   *Exporting Workers: The Turkish Case.* London: Cambridge University Press.

Peattie, Lisa
   1977   Introduction to Migrants and Women who Wait. *Signs* 3:126–27.

Pereira Neto, João
   1972   A Familia e a sociedade portuguese perante a industrialização. *Communidades portugueses* 7:4–25.

Pescatello, Ann
   1969   Both Ends of the Journey: An Historical Study of Migration and Change in Brazil and Portugal 1889–1914. Unpublished Ph.D. Dissertation, UCLA.

   1976   *Power and Pawn: The Female in Iberian Families, Societies, and Cultures.* Westport: Greenwood Press.

Picão, Jose Silva
   1947   *Através dos campos:* usos e costumes agricolos alentejanos. Lisbon: Neogravura Limitada.

Pinheiro, J., ed.
  np *La Saudade*. Lisbon.

Piore, Michael J.
  1979 *Birds of Passage: Migrant Labor and Industrial Societies*. Cambridge: Cambridge University Press.

Pitt, Rivers, Julian
  1954 *People of the Sierra*. London: Weidenfeld and Nicolson.

  1966 Honor and Social Status. In *Honor and Shame: The Values of Mediterranean Society*, edited by J.G. Peristiany, pp. 19–78. Chicago: University of Chicago Press.

Plotnicov, Leo
  1967 *Strangers to the City: Urban Man in Jos, Nigeria*. Pittsburgh: University of Pittsburgh Press.

Price, Richard and Sally Price
  1966 Noviazgo in an Andalusian Pueblo. *Southwestern Journal of Anthropology* 22:302–22.

Radin, Paul
  1926 *Crashing Thunder: The Autobiography of an American Indian*. New York: Appleton Publications (Dover Publications, 1963).

Reiter, Rayna
  1975 Men and Women in the South of France: Public and Private Domains. In *Toward an Anthropology of Women*, edited by Rayna Reiter, pp. 252–82. New York: Monthly Review Press.

Rhoades, Robert
  1979 From Caves to Main Street: Return Migration and the Transformation of a Spanish Village. *Papers in Anthropology* 20:57–74.

Riegelhaupt, Joyce
  1968 Saloio Women: An Analysis of Informal and Formal Political and Economic Roles of Portuguese Peasant Women. *Anthropological Quarterly* 40:109–26.

Rodrigues, Edgar, and Roberto das Neves
  1959 *A Fome em Portugal*. Rio de Janeiro: Editora Germinal.

Rogers, Susan
  1975 Female Forms of Power and the Myth of Male Dominance: A Model of Female-Male Interaction in Peasant Society. *American Ethnologist* 2:727–56.

  1976 The Great Escape: Women and Migration in the Aveyron. Paper presented to the 75th Annual Meeting of the American Anthropological Association. Washington, D.C.

  1978 Women's Place: A Critical Review of Anthropological Theory. *Comparative Studies in Society and History* 20:123–62.

Rosaldo, Michelle
  1974 Women, Culture and Society: A Theoretical Overview. In *Women, Cultural and Society*, edited by Louise Lamphere and Michelle Rosaldo, pp. 17–42. Stanford: Stanford University Press.

Rose, Arnold M.
  1969 *Migrants in Europe: Problems of Acceptance and Adjustment*. Minneapolis: University of Minnesota Press.

Sabisi, Harriet
  1977 How African Women Cope with Migrant Labor in South Africa. *Signs* 3:167–77.

Sanday, Peggy
  1973 Toward a Theory of the Status of Women. *American Anthropologist* 75:1682–700.

Schneider, Jane
  1971 Of Vigilance of Virgins: Honor, Shame, and Access to Resources in Mediterranean Societies. *Ethnology* 10:1–24.

Scott, Joan, and Louise Tilly
  1975 Women's Work and the Family in 19th Century Europe. *Comparative Studies in Society and History* 17:36–64.

Segalen, Maxime
  1973 Mari et femme dans la France rurale traditionnelle. Paris: Musée des Arts et Traditions Populaires.

Serrão, Joel
1974   Emigração portuguesa. Lisbon: Livros Horizonte, Colleção Horizonte #12.

Sheper-Hughes, Nancy
1979   Inheritance of the Meek: Land, Labor, and Love in Western Ireland, Marxist Perspectives 2:46–77.

1979a Breeding Breaks out in the Eye of the Cat: Sex Roles, Birth Order, and the Irish Double-Bind. Journal of Comparative Family Structure 10:207–26.

Shorter, Edward
1971   Illegitimacy, Sexual Deviance, and Social Change in Modern Europe. In The Family in History, edited by Theodore Rabb and Robert Rotberg, pp. 48–84. New York: Harper and Row.

Silva, Fernando Emygidio da
1917   Emigração portuguesa. Lisbon.

Simmons, Leo W.
1942   Sun Chief: The Autobiography of a Hopi Indian. New Haven: Yale University Press.

Smith, Margo
1971   Institutionalized Servitude: The Female Domestic in Lima Peru. Ph.D. Dissertation, Indiana University.

Sousa Ferreira, Eduardo
1976   Origens e formas da emigração. Lisbon: Iniciativas Editoriais.

Tapinos, Georges
1975   L'Immigration etrangère en France, 1946–73. Cahier no. 71, Travaux et Documents. Paris: Institut National des Études Demographiques.

Valle, Carlos
1967   Tradições do casamento. Comunidades Portugueses 6–8:91–196.

Vasconcellos, Carolina Michaelis
1922   A Saudade portuguesa. Lisbon.

Vernier Contrepied, V.
1956   Charme et sagesse du Portugal. Paris: Flammarion.

Willems, Emilio
  1962 On Portuguese Family Structure. *International Journal of Comparative Sociology* 3:65–79.

Wisniewski, Jean
  1974 Les Travailleurs Immigrés: Panorama Statistique. Paris: Hommes et Migrations, Documents #862.

Wolf, Margery
  1969 *Women and Family in Rural Taiwan.* Stanford: Stanford University Press.